Toward
Octavio Paz

Toward
Octavio Paz
A Reading of
His Major Poems
1957-1976

JOHN M. FEIN

THE UNIVERSITY PRESS OF KENTUCKY

Scholarly publisher for the Commonwealth,
serving Bellarmine College, Berea College, Centre
College of Kentucky, Eastern Kentucky University,
The Filson Club, Georgetown College, Kentucky
Historical Society, Kentucky State University,
Morehead State University, Murray State University,
Northern Kentucky University, Transylvania University,
University of Kentucky, University of Louisville,
and Western Kentucky University.

Editorial and Sales Offices: Lexington, Kentucky 40506-0024

Library of Congress Cataloging-in-Publication Data
Fein, John M., 1922-
   Toward Octavio Paz.

   Bibliography: p.
   Includes index.
   1. Paz, Octavio, 1914-   —Criticism and
interpretation. I. Title.
PQ7297.P285Z727 1986   861   85-29417
ISBN 0-8131-1569-8

To the memory of Amado Alonso,
whose seminar opened students' eyes
to poetry in Spanish

Contents

Acknowledgments

I am deeply indebted to three friends who were generous with their time and helpful in their suggestions for improving the manuscript: Professors Andrew Debicki of the University of Kansas, Wallace Fowlie of Duke University, and James Holloway of Dalhousie University. The criticism and encouragement of my son, David, a professor at the University of North Carolina at Greensboro, make me both humble and proud. I can only hope that this book responds to some of their recommendations successfully.

Note on Texts

Unless otherwise indicated, I have relied on the latest edition of Paz's collected poetry (*Poemas*, 1979) for references to his texts. In order to minimize quotations, I have assumed that my readers will have the texts at hand and that they may wish to number the lines. Chapters 4, 6, and 7 (except for "A vista de pájaro," "Palabras en forma de tolvanera," and "Anotaciones / Rotaciones") utilize the translations of *Configurations* and *A Draft of Shadows*, for which I thank their publisher, New Directions. All other translations are my own.

1 Introduction

The title of this book is derived from two studies by Professor Harry Levin that were popular about forty years ago when I was a college student. *Toward Stendhal* and *Toward Balzac* suggest an attitude of modesty before a literary giant. Even more important is the implication that every great writer we study is to some degree unattainable, no matter how clear or moving his literary creation may be. This incompleteness, which is perhaps more the reader's than the author's, is particularly applicable in the case of Octavio Paz, whose poetic goal is the expression of what he feels to be basically incommunicable. The reader, therefore, can only approach the author's work and accept with mystery, frustration, or pleasure the realization that his comprehension will be imperfect.

The undisputed intellectual leadership of Paz, not only in Mexico but throughout Spanish America, rests on a dichotomy of achievements. In the field of the essay, he is the author of twenty-five books on subjects whose diversity—esthetics, politics, Surrealist art, the Mexican character, cultural anthropology, and Eastern philosophy, to cite only a few—is dazzling. In twenty-one books of poetry spanning more than fifty years, his creativity has increased in vigor as he has explored the numerous possibilities opened to Hispanic poets from many different sources. His success in diversified fields is heightened by the ways in which his essays and his poetry are complementary: the core of his creativity is a concern for language in general and for the poetic process in particular.

Like most intellectuals, Paz is more the result of his rigorous inquiry and self-discipline than of an educational system. The family into which he was born in Mexico City in 1914 represented, in its combination of indigenous and Spanish heritage and of Catholicism and nonbelief, and in its impoverishment after the Revolution, the history of his country. As a child he led a rather solitary life in a crumbling mansion and attended a French religious school, having been tutored in that language by an aunt. He had access to his grandfather's library, which introduced him to Latin, Greek, and Spanish classics, nineteenth-century French authors, and writers in Spanish who were popular around the turn of the century.[1]

At fourteen he showed the dedication to poetry and the autodidacticism that were to shape his life. Although his family persuaded him to attend the schools of Arts and Letters and Law at the university, he did not receive a degree. His enthusiasm for poetry turned to the Spanish generation of 1927; only later did he discover their predecessors of the post-modernist period. At nineteen, when he published his first book of poems, *Luna silvestre*, Paz was an active member of literary groups, a contributor to literary reviews, and the founder of two. He was in the center of a productive and eclectic activity that introduced the most innovative French, English, and Spanish writers to Mexico.

A key event in Paz's life was the invitation, at the suggestion of Pablo Neruda, to attend a congress of anti-fascist writers in Spain in 1937. At the height of the Civil War, he met not only the leading Spanish writers (Cernuda, Alberti, Altolaguirre, Antonio Machado), but also Spanish Americans (Neruda, Huidobro, Vallejo). An even more important result of the experience in Spain was the feeling of solidarity, which Paz was to call, in another context, "communion."

He continued to express that feeling in his work on behalf of Spanish Republicans, particularly those in exile in Mexico, and in his collaboration in *El popular*, a politically oriented newspaper sponsored by Mexican workers. In 1940 he broke with *El popular* and with Neruda as a result of the Russian-German pact. His literary prestige grew through his contributions to three literary journals (*Taller*, 1938; *Tierra nueva*, 1940; and *El hijo pródigo*, 1943) and his role in the introduction of Surrealism to Mexico.

With the support of a Guggenheim grant in 1944, Paz visited the United States, where he began the brilliant essay on Mexican character, *El laberinto de la soledad* [*The Labyrinth of Solitude*], that was to attract international attention when it was published in 1950. The first edition of his collected poetry, *Libertad bajo palabra*, appeared in 1949. His appointment to the diplomatic service took him to Paris, where he strengthened his knowledge of, and connection with, French writers, particularly Breton and the Surrealists.

Roggiano defines the period from 1951 to 1968 as Paz's most productive and complex.[2] Not only does it mark his creative and intellectual maturity (eight books of poetry and seven of essays), but also a rise in his diplomatic career, culminating in six years as head of the Mexican Embassy in India. The years in India also brought him personal fulfillment in his second marriage. Above all, Paz became, in both his life and his work, a truly international figure.

The massacre of students at Tlatelolco in 1968, for which the Mexican government was responsible, was a turning point in Paz's life. His immediate response was a short but eloquent poem in protest and the submission of his resignation from the diplomatic service. He accepted several short academic appointments at the universities of Cambridge, Pittsburgh, and Texas, and in 1971-72 the Charles Eliot Norton Chair at Harvard. His success there led to a regular appointment as Professor of Comparative Literature until 1980, when he retired and was recognized by Harvard with an honorary degree. During these years he directed a lively literary supplement in Mexico, *Plural*. After political maneuvering forced him and most of *Plural*'s contributing staff to resign, he founded another journal, *Vuelta*, which is generally regarded today as the best of its kind in Latin America.

Paz's numerous books of essays offer ample evidence of his productivity as a thinker. Just as the meaning of history underlies his analyses of society, so does the significance of language connect his numerous essays on Hispanic and French poetry and art. Ranging from *El arco y la lira* (1956)—a brilliant interpretation of poetry as language, process, and social phenomenon—to his broad history of the evolution of modern poetry, *Los hijos del limo: Del romanticismo a la vanguardia* (1974) [*Children of the Mire: Modern Poetry from Romanticism to the Avant-Garde*], he views the distillation of language not as an adornment of mankind but as a key to its comprehension. His seminal study of the French artist, *Marcel Duchamp o el castillo de la pureza* (1968) [*Marcel Duchamp, or the Castle of Purity*], provides insights into contemporary hermetic expression, including his own work. The massive *Sor Juana Inés de la Cruz, o, Las trampas de la fe* (1982) is equally revolutionary in its scholarship on the remarkable philosopher, scientist, and authoress, and in its intellectual history of the Colonial period.

Paz's poetry and prose represent two aspects of a concern for the predicament of modern man, whom he is not unique in viewing as fragmented and mutilated. In fact, all of his work is unified by a utopian wish for the fulfillment of man's wholeness in individual creativity and in the building of society, offering an ennobling vision of man to an uneasy world. This vision underlies his attempts to reconcile opposites, especially those of passion and reason, linear and circular time, society and the individual, and word and meaning.

My interest in Paz's poetry began before 1956, when I published an article that may have the merit of being the first extensive critical essay in English on his work. Since that time I have read his books eagerly and analyzed his poems enthusiastically with my students at Duke University. I cannot claim that I have understood completely what I have studied; Paz's complexity, illuminated so well by Carlos H. Magis in *La poesía hermética de Octavio Paz*, always leaves something to be explored. In providing explication of most of the longer poems published between 1957 and 1976 (from *Piedra de sol* through *Vuelta*), my principal objective is to help those not acquainted with Paz's poetry to surmount initial difficulties in order to respond personally to his voice. I hope also that scholars may find these new readings useful, or at least that they may understand my response to poems that move me in varied and sometimes puzzling ways.

My basic approach is to study the interrelationship of the parts of the poem, particularly structure and theme, integral to a close reading of the texts. This is not an easy task for Paz's work or indeed for any poet whose major production has appeared in the last fifty years. The development of poetry in all Western languages away from conventional form seems to have diminished the usefulness of the New Criticism. Nonetheless, that method is productive as a point of departure for understanding contemporary poets, and has the advantage of providing a link with the poetry of earlier generations in showing how traditional devices such as structure, tone, metaphor, and symbolism can be used in innovative ways.

Since Magis' study cited above covers the early period of Paz's poetry thoroughly, I have concentrated on the major poems and collections after *La estación violenta* in the present work. The only exception is the first chapter, on *Piedra de sol*, a revised version of my article "La estructura de 'Piedra de sol,' " which appeared in the *Revista iberoamericana*. Its approach to the poem as a whole differs considerably from Magis' methodology. Separate chapters here are dedicated to two other lengthy works that Paz published separately, *Blanco* and *Pasado en claro*. The three chapters on collections of poems, those on *Salamandra*, *Ladera este*, and *Vuelta*, focus on long poems that can be considered characteristic of these volumes.

My chapter titles suggest Paz's different but complementary attempts to expand the reader's sensitivity to poetry. They are labels of dominant, rather than exclusive, approaches. The polarities of *Ladera este*, for example, can be found in much of the poetry before and after its publication. *Blanco*, likewise, anticipates *Pasado en claro* by including the poem itself as part of the subject, and all the major poems lead to silence through truncations of the text. The chapter titles, accordingly, emphasize the primary technique of each of the volumes studied in order to delineate Paz's efforts to create a more responsive reader.

There are two major characteristics of Paz's work that are particularly challenging to his critics. The first is his relationship to the Surrealists, among whom French poets figure more significantly than their Hispanic counterparts. It is obvious that Paz, who is trilingual in Spanish, English, and French, feels a great affinity with French culture and history of ideas. His veneration of André Breton, for example, clearly delineated in Jason Wilson's excellent book, suggests that his affiliation with Surrealism is part of the origin of his hermeticism. The difficulties for the critic are obvious: how can one define the theme of a poem that is so intensely personal that its ultimate definition rests within the text itself? How can one assume a common response from readers when the poem in fact invites multiple responses, each of which is justifiable and may conflict with, if not exclude, the alternate readings?

Another significant critical problem is posed by Paz's concept of poetry, which has developed over the period of many years and can be seen most clearly in his essays. These, as has often been observed, are the basis for comparing him to the late Alfonso Reyes, not only in their breadth and brilliance, but particularly in their contribution to critical theory and to an understanding of the role of poetry in society. Paz's first effort in this field, "Poesía de comunión y poesía de soledad," is as meaningful today as when it first appeared in *El hijo pródigo* in 1943. Some of the ideas outlined there were the nucleus for the best developed and most readable volume on poetic theory that Latin America has produced, *El arco y la lira* (1956). The observation of Paz's evolution as a critic is in itself an educational process. Paz himself is the first to note rectifications and clarifications (see Rodríguez Monegal's article on the differences between the editions of *El arco y la lira*), but the concepts underlying his theories remain basically unchanged. Central to his critical thought are the desire to make poetry more meaningful to man and the conviction that poetry must go beyond the text to (and through) the individual's response. The essence of the poem, he believes, is unwritten, and therefore silent. It is analogous to the pauses in musical composition that express as much meaning as the sounds. If the poem ends in silence, the critic is reluctant to intrude with his own interpretation of meaning.

The constants of Paz's concept of poetry can be stated in a series of paradoxes. The poet writes only for himself but must communicate to an audience. The poem is a mystery whose creation can never be accurately described, yet man cannot receive it without thinking about the process that created it.

Language is a defective but indispensable instrument for conveying what is incommunicable. Poetry is an ecstasy that both denies and transforms reality; although it cannot be grasped, it is essential to man's concept of himself and to the functioning of society. Perhaps the most troublesome of Paz's paradoxes is his rejection of analysis as an aid to understanding contemporary poetry. Even his notes to *Ladera este*, limited to geographical and historical explanations, are regarded by Paz with reluctance and suspicion:

> Como en algunos pasajes aparecen palabras y alusiones a personas, ideas y cosas que podrían extrañar al lector no familiarizado con esa región del mundo, varios amigos me aconsejaron incluir, al final de este volumen, unas cuantas notas que aclarasen esas oscuridades—y otras no menos superfluas. Los obedezco, con el temor (¿la esperanza?) de que estas notas, lejos de disiparlos, aumenten los enigmas.[3]

> [Since in some passages there appear words and allusions to people, ideas, and things that might puzzle the reader who is not familiar with that part of the world, several friends advised me to include at the end of this volume a few notes to clear up those difficulties—and others not less superfluous. I accede to them with the fear (hope?) that these notes, far from dissipating the enigmas, will increase them.]

It is significant that the notes are omitted in the collected poetry of *Poemas*. A more important distrust of critical interpretation appears in Paz's essay "Hablar y decir," in which he supports Maistre's observation that thought and word are synonymous and Breton's similar belief that poetry is the perfect equivalence between sound and meaning, rendering any further statement superfluous. It is, Paz maintains, meaningless to ask what a poem means: "Los poemas no se explican ni se interpretan; en ellos el signo cesa de significar: es" [Poems cannot be explained or interpreted; in them the sign stops signifying: it is]. The

8   Toward Octavio Paz

clearest summary of Paz's anticritical stance is the conclusion of his introduction to *Poesía en movimiento:* "La significación de la poesía, si alguna tiene, no está ni en los juicios del crítico ni en las opiniones del poeta. La significación es cambiante y momentánea: brota del encuentro entre el poema y el lector" [The meaning of poetry, if it has any, is neither in the judgments of the critic nor in the opinions of the poet. The meaning is changing and momentary: it comes from the encounter between the poem and the reader].

The diminishment, if not the elimination, of criticism's role in understanding poetry results in increased responsibilities for the reader. In the same way that contemporary drama experiments with the location of the stage and with the distinction between actors and audience to abolish the latter's passivity, so does Paz seek to enable the reader not only to respond to the poem, but to assist in its creation. His objective is to reduce the differences between poet and reader, so that the two can work together in a common purpose. He is aware, of course, of the paradoxical nature of his mission: just as to reach ultimate expression he must abolish words, so must the reader and poet communicate by transcending the poem. As early as 1938, Paz referred to "el lector de poesía, que cada día más es un verdadero reconstructor de ella" [the reader of poetry who is more and more a true reconstructor of it]. In recent years he has developed this concept to its logical conclusion, transforming the reader into a poet by confronting him with demanding literature: "According to this view of reader participation, the interpretive act becomes synonymous with the creative process itself."[4]

In her very perceptive essay, Ruth Needleman traces the origin of Paz's concept of the reader to the fundamental change in his view of language that took place between the two editions of *El arco y la lira* in 1956 and 1967. In the first he denied the possibility of separating language from its human context. In the second he notes the loss of that context and the substitution of a multiplicity of meanings: "Coherence, as a result, has ceded its place to fragmentation, so that the meaning, no longer immanent, resides in the very search for meaning." The poem, consequently, becomes variable according to the experience and the capacity of the reader: "The meanings are inherent in the poem, and the reader realizes them by rendering them conscious." Whether the average person can measure up to this responsibility is a serious question that Needleman answers indirectly.[5]

Paz's poetry is consistent with his theories in the multiple possibilities it presents for interpretation. The reader who is not acquainted with those theories may feel that the poems are inconclusive, or even unconcluded, presented as sketches or notes. If he persists, however, he will understand that the poet invites him to feel his own version of the poem. Brotherston's statement in *Latin American Poetry* that Paz is "a poet of movement, defined by successive moments" succinctly classifies not the end of the reader's response but the beginning.[6] Paz's description of Duchamp's work as the bridge between the polarities of the absence of meaning and the necessity of meaning is helpful in comprehending his own intentions.[7] Perhaps more clearly than any other critic, Gabriel Zaid has urged us to have new objectives:

> Examinada con rigor, la obra de Octavio Paz no entrega significaciones últimas. No es una obra derivada de últimas instancias, sino surgida en el lugar de origen de las últimas instancias. La última significación de la obra de Paz no es una significación, es un acto vivo: moverse y movernos al lugar de las últimas significaciones.[8]
>
> [When one examines it carefully, the work of Octavio Paz does not yield ultimate meanings. It is not a work derived from ultimate demands, but originating at the source of the ultimate demands. The final meaning of Paz's work is not a meaning but a living act: to move itself and to move us to the place of the final meanings.]

In addition to the constants noted by critics (the desire for transcendence, the symbolism of the paradox, the quest for origins, and the polarities of solitude and communion), there is one less documented constant: Paz's attempts to shape through his poetry a more sensitive, independent, and enlightened reader. This is an additional goal for a poet who assigns a high priority to forging a new—or at least clearer—medium of communication. One feels that in Paz the order of urgency is, if not reversed, simultaneous. He would not be satisfied to write a different kind of poetry unless he had the hope that it would create a reader with a different set of expectations. *Toward Octavio Paz* attempts to clarify the ways in which the poet helps the reader not only to define these expectations but to achieve them.

2 *Piedra de sol*
The Divided Circle

lo que pasó no fue pero está siendo
y silenciosamente desemboca
en otro instante que se desvanece:

[what happened did not take place but is taking place
and silently empties
into another moment that vanishes:]
—Paz, *Piedra de sol*

The acclamation of the critics, which presented *Piedra de sol* as a masterpiece from the outset, is justified by its continued popularity. Almost thirty years after its publication, it stands above Paz's other early works, not so much for its Mexican character (in spite of the title's reference to the massive Aztec calendar stone) as for the universality of its comprehension both of man's yearning and of his finiteness. This long poem is essentially a quest (or, as Phillips expresses it, a pilgrimage) in which the unnamed voice attempts to define his identity. The interpretations of the search may vary, but its significance is felt by all. Pacheco's personal tribute, borrowing Cyril Connolly's judgment of Ezra Pound, represents the critical consensus: he wants three copies of Paz's work—to read, reread, and be buried with.[1]

The subject of *Piedra de sol* ostensibly is love, or, more particularly, the beloved. Phillips interprets the poem as a search for woman, and notes the metaphors that link her to Nature, menacing but regenerative, the unifier of opposites and the reconciler of antagonisms.[2] The quest is not a search for love so much as an attempt to define it by the voice (who is different from the poet). The "narrative" of the poem, therefore, is not only constantly symbolic, but also a combination of what is most personal and universal.

If one looks beyond the experience of love, the real subject of the poem is time and its relationship to reality. In describing his own feelings of love and those of lovers in general, the poem's speaker attempts to define transience and permanence, illusion and reality. Love is, therefore, metaphysics. Gimferrer expresses the significance of this objective with concision: "Queda claro, pues, que de lo que aquí se trata es de asediar, de poner cerco al instante, en busca de su fijeza en el poema, que nos revelará nuestro verdadero ser"[3] [It remains clear, then, that what is dealt with here is besieging, surrounding the moment, in search of its permanence in the poem, which will reveal our true being to ourselves].

All critics comment on the circularity of the poem—the repetition of the six introductory verses as its conclusion—and its implication for a nonlinear concept of time. Pacheco and Phillips, in addition, see a progression in the experiences of the poem, so that they constitute a spiral rather than a circle. Phillips adds the significant observation that the point of departure is not the same, for it has been "transformed by the experience which is the poem itself."[4] The details of structure that are the subject of the present chapter, particularly the relationship between the poem's halves, the connection wth the pre-Columbian calendar, and the pattern of episodes and reflections, are keys to the poem's theme.

The polarization of the two orientations of Paz's poetry, the personal and the universal, emerges most clearly in *Piedra de sol.* The poem is preceded by an epigraph, the first verses of Gérard de Nerval's "Artémis," and followed by an explanatory note in which Paz gives an explicit clue—unique in his work to date—to the poem's interpretation, based on the cycles of a pre-Columbian calendar. The opposition of these two keys, which are integral to the poem's theme of time but extrinsic to its form, is the foundation of the work.

"Artémis" is one of the best known works of the relatively limited poetic production of Nerval. It is at the same time among the most enigmatic poems by this generally puzzling forerunner of Symbolism and Surrealism. In fact, the number of analytical interpretations of "Artémis" continuing to the present are eloquent evidence of its relevance to the reading

public. Nor can one safely predict that the final judgment of
this obscure combination of mythology, Christianity, and
personal symbolism has been formulated, for there are likely
to be further theories about its meaning. Perhaps every crit-
ical interpretation counteracts the author's intention; Nerval
himself was the first to warn that the essence of the poem
might be lost if it were explained.

Its opening quatrain has been clarified by critical commen-
tary more frequently than the rest of the poem:

La treizième revient . . . c'est encore la première;
Et c'est toujours la seule—ou c'est le seul moment;
Car es-tu reine, ô toi, la première ou dernière?
Es-tu roi, toi le seul ou le dernier amant?

[The thirteenth returns . . . it is still the first;
And it is always the only one—or it is the only moment;
For are you, queen, you, the first or last?
Are you, king, the only or the last lover?]

Certainly the basic identification of the number thirteen
here is with the hour. Nerval himself made this clear, not
only in the subtitle of one of his manuscripts, "Ballet des
heures" [Dance of the Hours], but also in a marginal note of
another: "La XIIIe heure (pivotale)"[5] [The thirteenth hour
(turning point)]. Yet there must be more than one con-
notation in a major poem by a writer who influenced both
Baudelaire and Mallarmé.

Several commentators have sought a biographical signifi-
cance to the number thirteen. More important is the hypoth-
esis that Nerval composed his poem on the first day of 1854
(which would make it the thirteenth-first month as well as
hour).[6] Nerval's biographers also emphasize his deep convic-
tion that his destiny was ruled by the stars, and Richer's
detailed study testifies to the poet's reliance on numerology,
cabalism, and a variety of symbolic and numerical oc-
cultisms.[7]

The most concrete connection between time and Artemis,
apart from the various symbolisms of the moon, may have

been unknown to Paz when he wrote *Piedra de sol.* In any
case, its meaning was so personal to Nerval that the average
modern reader could not be expected to break its hermetic
character. Jean Onimus appropriately comments that his ex-
planation "décevra par sa simplicité les amateurs de sym-
bolisme" [will disappoint the devotees of symbolism by its
simplicity]. Apparently Nerval's title recalled his vivid im-
pression of an ornate Renaissance pendulum clock in which
the figure of time was supported by caryatids:

> La Diane historique, accoudée à son cerf, est en bas-
> relief sous le cadran où s'étalent sur un fond niellé les
> chiffres émaillés des heures. . . . Les anciens cadrans
> portent au-dessus des chiffres 1, 2, 3, etc., les numéros
> 13, 14, 15, etc. L'équation 1 = 13 s'impose ainsi au
> premier regard. Cette Diane accoudée sous le cadran
> semble, détachée de l'éternelle ronde des heures, man-
> ifester la sérénité du divin, en contraste avec cette figure
> du Temps qui dominait l'édifice. La précision des détails
> montre à quel point Nerval en 1853, dix-huit ans plus
> tard, garde l'exacte mémoire d'un objet qu'il a longue-
> ment contemplé et qui, sans doute, l'a fait rêver. Diane
> devient ainsi pour lui le symbole même du Temps.[8]

[The traditional Diana, leaning on her stag, is in relief
on the dial, on which the enameled numbers of the
hours are ranged on an inlaid background. . . . Old dials
show below the numbers 1, 2, 3, etc., the numbers 13, 14,
15, etc. The equation 1 = 13 is thus obvious at the first
glance. This Diana leaning under the dial, separated
from the eternal round of the hours, seems to express a
divine serenity, in contrast to the figure of Time that
dominates the construction. The precision of the details
show to what extent Nerval in 1853, eighteen years
later, keeps the exact recall of an object which he looked
at for a long time and which he certainly must have
dreamed of. Diana thus becomes for him the very sym-
bol of Time.]

In its point of departure, at least, the association of Diana-Artemis with time is as personal for Nerval as it is concrete in its identification with the clock. Its significance for Paz is obviously not the mythological association but the circular aspect of time, which Onimus designates as the equation 1 = 13.[9] This circular aspect is continually suggested in *Piedra de sol* by the use of the comma to replace all other punctuation except for the colon. The colon, significantly, is used in conjunction with a hemistich to express vividly the combination of break and continuity in thirteen places.

In addition to the theme of time, there are two other related features of "Artémis" that contribute to the comprehension of Paz's poem. Richer has commented on the thirteen names of Isis, significant not only for the equivalence in Nerval's number of hours, but also for the multiplicity of the goddess's identity. Another critic shows the hidden identity of Isis behind Artemis, and wonders, since Isis when appearing to a worshipper would show him the face of his beloved, whether Nerval was not reversing the process and seeking the goddess in the faces of several women.[10] Richer applies two quotations from *Aurélia* to demonstrate convincingly that in Nerval's mind Isis becomes the Virgin and a mother figure and Venus: "Isis est dite déesse polymorphe, déesse aux mille noms"[11] [Isis is said to be a goddess of many forms, the goddess of a thousand names]. The same multiplicity of symbols applies in *Piedra de sol* to the goddess of time, who is invoked particularly at the conclusion of the poem.

Another application of the epigraph is seen in the use of "première," "dernière," and "seul," all terms in opposition normally, but really intended as synonyms in this poetic context. The play of opposites is developed extensively in the quatrains of "Artémis"; in fact, only the eighth verse lacks an explicit contrast of terms. The sonnet's final lines contain the great contrast that embodies and explains all the others. A similar use of paradox, both in theme and metaphor, is one of the characteristic features of *Piedra de sol*.

Paz's note to the first edition (1957) represents the opposite pole of the poem's orientation. One wonders why this brief but revealing commentary was omitted from the definitive collection of *Libertad bajo palabra*. Did Paz feel that it revealed too much? Did readers misinterpret its purpose? Did the note tend to distort the public's response to a major creative work?

The note explains the importance of the Mayan hieroglyphic on the cover by translating its meaning as 585, and adds that pictorial symbols marking the beginning and end correspond to Día 4 Olín [Movement] and Día 4 Ehécatl [Wind]. The number of hendecasyllables, 584 (not counting the reprise in verses 585-90), corresponds to the synodic cycle of Venus. Since Venus appears both as morning and as evening star, its duality has been impressed on men as the symbol of the universe's essential ambiguity. In the same way, Ehécatl was one of the forms of Quetzalcoatl, the plumed serpent who represents the two sides of life. Venus, for the Western world, was a complex association of images and ambivalent forces (Ishtar, the Wife of the Sun, the Conic Stone, the Unsculptured Stone, Aphrodite, the quadruple Venus of Cicero, the double goddess of Pausanias, and others).

In spite of the opposition of the epigraph and the poet's note, they have a numerical link in common. The number 13 is both the symbol of time's circularity for Nerval and the number of months in the lunar reckoning of the Aztec calendar (260 days, comprising 13 months of 20 days each, to which were added 105 days of solar reckoning to fill out the solar year). In this way, too, the thirteen lunar months of the solar year in the European calendar are linked with the lunar reckoning of the Aztec calendar. Thus the mathematical calculations of moon time reinforce subtly but unmistakably the symbol of the moon as defined by Nerval in the poem's point of departure. The number 13 plays other roles in the Aztec calendar. Their week, for example, consists of thirteen days. Counting each year in turn, thirteen years are dominated by the four directional points in a "century" of 52 years. The century is divided into four series of thirteen years, each of which is also dominated by a cardinal point.

Midway between the epigraph and the poet's note on the Aztec calendar is the poem's most significant structural element, the line—or rather, poetic label—"Madrid, 1937." At first glance this simply marks a change of subject and tone. The reader senses, however, that the label may also designate one of the most climactic experiences in the poet's life outside the poem. Paz confirms the philosophical significance of this experience in an autobiographical paragraph of *El laberinto de la soledad*:

> Recuerdo que en España, durante la guerra, tuve la revelación de "otro hombre" y de otra clase de soledad: ni cerrada ni maquinal, sino abierta a la transcendencia.[12]

> [I remember that in Spain, during the war, I had the revelation of "another man" and of another kind of solitude: neither closed nor mechanical, but open to transcendence.]

Paz is aware that many parts of the Spanish dream were shattered, but the memory of that ideal has become part of his character, his destiny, and his aspirations:

> Pero su recuerdo no me abandona. Quien ha visto la Esperanza, no la olvida. La busca bajo todos los cielos y entre todos los hombres. Y sueña que un día va a encontrarla de nuevo, no sabe dónde, acaso entre los suyos. En cada hombre late la posibilidad de ser, o más exactamente, *de volver a ser*, otro hombre.[13]

> [But its memory never leaves me. Whoever has seen Hope does not forget it. He looks for it under all skies and among all men. And he dreams that one day he is going to find it again, he does not know where, perhaps among his own people. In each man there lives the possibility of being, or more precisely, *of being again*, another man.]

Clearly the designation of Madrid, 1937, can be interpreted as a watershed, dividing the poet's life in two.

The transcendence of the biographical experience is reflected in the poem's structure. "Madrid, 1937" is prominent first for its place in the poem, between verses 287 and 288, only five lines distant from the exact arithmetical center. Although it would be a perfect hendecasyllabic verse written out, it draws attention not only as a verse that the poet did not count in the total of 584, but also because it is an obvious unmusical intrusion in the rhythmic circularity. The impact of the break is reinforced by the poet's refusal to place a period before the change of scene to mark the conclusion of the first half of the poem, using commas before and after as he does throughout the poem. The label of time and place, paradoxically, is a break that is not a break.

In a similar fashion the reader can make a comparison and contrast between the two halves of the poem. Both represent a quest for meaning in life; both involve, as we shall see, the repetition of a basic experience, although the experiences of the two halves are opposites; both describe the circularity of time. In general terms, the subject of both halves is the same. There is a fundamental opposition, however, in direction and tone. We recall that the epigraph suggests a metaphysical analysis of the number thirteen as first, last, and/or the same, and/or stationary within time. By raising specifically, in two interrogations, the implications of first or last, along with the question of identity (queen or king), Nerval starts a chain reaction of doubts that proceed inward. The reader is led to react subjectively, as the poet has, to the questioning of time and reality. The first half of *Piedra de sol* generally follows the same inward direction. The poet's quest is within his soul, a voyage into the depths of his own identity as he strives to define an ultimate reality.

Just as the poem's first half is oriented around the epigraph, the second is dominated by the direction of the poet's note at the end. By combining science and myth, the note relies not on the psyche, but on collective creativity and measurable phenomena. Its orientation, therefore, is outward. The second half of the poem, following this orientation, describes reality in social terms: war, love, human aspirations, and

society's problems. Where the tone of the first half is se-
cretive, the dominant tone of the second is open. Using the
phrases that Paz used in another and broader context, we
might say that the first half is "poesía de la soledad" [poetry of
solitude] and the second is "poesía de la comunión" [poetry of
communion].
This distinction should not suggest that each half is uni-
fied in its opposition to the other. On the contrary, we shall
see that the reverse is true: the poet planned "intrusions" of
the first in the second and of the second in the first. The
difference in orientation should be defined in terms of a
domination that deliberately includes examples of its op-
posite.

Although the theme of *Piedra de sol* is the relationship
between time and reality, the significance of terms associated
with time is narrow. Paz's use of "minuto," "hora," or, pre-
ferably, "instante," tends to be concrete, leaving the broader
symbolism to other features of the poem. Even the normally
abstract "tiempo," with the notable exception of verses
189-99, applies to a particular situation or to a fleeting per-
sonal reaction rather than to wide philosophical speculation.
Seldom in the use of time words does one find an explicit
justification for the circularity symbolized by the poem's
title and developed by its structure.

An examination of the various references to time yields
common denominators and suggests three general cassifica-
tions: normal or "standard" time; time as measured by the
poet's experience; and timelessness as a characteristic of
eternity. The decor of the surrealistic landscape that serves as
an introduction (15-16, 21, 31, etc.) includes references to time
that are easily accessible to the reader in a normal context.
Although these are prominent in the first part of the poem, as
if the poet wished to establish a broad base of common
understanding about time on which he could construct the
precarious tower of personal impressions and philosophical
concepts, they also occur in other sections:

> mientras afuera el tiempo se desboca [159]
> [while outside time runs out of control]

el mundo con su horario carnicero [161]
[the world with its bloodthirsty schedule]
mientras el tiempo cierra su abanico [171]
[while time closes its fan]
presente sin ventanas [225]
[windowless present]
pétalo de cristal es cada hora [401]
[each hour is a glass petal]
silencio: cruzó un ángel este instante [436]
[silence: an angel just went by]

Even near the conclusion, after the full development of nu-
merous subthemes and symbols, time is seen briefly in a very
normal guise: "se despeñó el instante en otro y otro" (572)
[the moment plunged into another and another].
The poet's concept of time as judged by his own experience
anticipates the circularity of the poem's structure. In one of
the invocations to his beloved, who has many names and
faces, the poet parallels directly the lines of the epigraph:
"tienes todos los rostros y ninguno, / eres todas las horas y
ninguna" (116-17) [you have all faces and none, / you are all
hours and none]. The development of this idea is expressed in
terms that unite the circularity of time with the concrete—
and hence temporary, since time changes everything—face of
the beloved:

rostro de llamas, rostro devorado,
adolescente rostro perseguido
años fantasmas, días circulares
que dan al mismo patio, al mismo muro,
arde el instante y son un solo rostro
los sucesivos rostros de la llama,
todos los nombres son un solo nombre,
todos los rostros son un solo rostro,
todos los siglos son un solo instante

> y por todos los siglos de los siglos
> cierra el paso al futuro un par de ojos,
> [142-52]
>
> [face of flames, devoured face,
> adolescent face pursued
> during phantom years, circular days
> that end in the same patio, the same wall,
> the moment burns and the successive faces
> of the flame are a single face,
> all the names are a single name,
> all the faces are a single face,
> all the centuries are a single moment
> and during all the eternal centuries
> the future is blocked by a pair of eyes,]

In the poet's most meaningful commentary on his experience of time, he stresses its circularity by the use of the present progressive tense, which transforms the linear concept of time into a paradoxical merging of past and present:

> oh vida por vivir y ya vivida,
> tiempo que vuelve en una marejada
> y se retira sin volver el rostro,
> lo que pasó no fue pero está siendo
> y silenciosamente desemboca
> en otro instante que se desvanece:
> [189-94]
>
> [oh life to be lived and already lived,
> time that returns in a wave
> and withdraws without turning its face,
> what happened did not take place but is taking place
> and silently empties
> into another moment that vanishes:]

Throughout the poem, there are other reminders that the circularity of time is a dilemma and a symbol of disorientation. Whether the present is meaningless because it is pro-

longed interminably, or whether events, both personal and
historical, lack significance because they are endlessly re-
peated, the poet's reaction to time's circularity is summed up
by verse 498, "cada minuto es nada para siempre" [each
minute is nothing forever]. The first verses of the last stanza
express his reaction to the dilemma:

> quiero seguir, ir más allá, y no puedo:
> se despeñó el instante en otro y otro
> [571-72]
>
> [I want to continue, to go farther, and I cannot:
> the moment plunged into another and another]

Considered against the background of normal time, linear
time that stretches in measured units both forward and back-
ward, is the poet's dominant concept of circular time an-
nounced by the epigraph. Yet the awareness of the moment
that is simultaneously first, last, and unique brings no resolu-
tion, peace, or realization. On the contrary, it implies to the
poet that there is an ultimate reality, a timeless realm, that he
searches for beyond all other realities, and that is intimated
by several experiences of love in the second half. The small
amount of space given to the concept of the timeless paradise
is in inverse relation to its importance as the poem's emo-
tional goal, which is defined in the penultimate stanza
(562-70). Above all other descriptions, this holds the most
abiding hope of a final fulfillment.

With the exception noted, the explicit references to time
do not develop it as a theme. They corroborate instead the
reader's own impression of its transitory and unreliable
nature, along with the difficulty of reaching a satisfactory
definition. The poem's contribution to a broader definition of
the relationship of time to reality is expressed not by time
words, but by the pattern—and particularly the repetition—
of the poet's experience. Before examining this pattern, we
should observe the use of the cardinal points of the compass,
which suggest that the poet's experience is a universal one.
The fusion of the concepts of time and space in Aztec

cosmology is quite different from their completely separate development in the European tradition:

> Enfin, de même qu'il n'y a pas un espace mais des espaces, il n'y a pas un temps mais des temps. De plus, chaque espace est lié à un temps, ou à des temps. Ainsi la mentalité mexicaine ne connaît pas l'espace et le temps abstraits, mais des sites et des événements. Les propriétés de chaque espace sont aussi celles du temps qui lui est attaché, et réciproquement. Tout phénomène du monde ou de la vie humaine prend place en un lieu et en un moment déterminés; sa tonalité, sa valeur émotionnelle, les prévisions qu'on en peut tirer pour l'avenir, dépendent de ce complexe singulier d'espace et de temps où il est apparu.[14]

> [Finally, just as there is not one space but several, so is there not one time but several. Moreover, each space is connected with a period or periods of time. Thus Mexican mentality does not know abstract time and space but rather places and events. The properties of each space are also those of the time that is connected with it, and vice versa. Every phenomenon of the world or of human life takes place at a certain place and time; its tonality, its emotional value, the suppositions that one can draw for the future, depend on this unique combination of time and space in which it appeared.]

Since the Aztec calendar cycle of fifty-two years always begins with 1 *acatl*, the year of the East, it indicates not only the beginning of our world, but also the birth of the sun and the dominance of Quetzalcoatl, who after he is sacrificed appears in the East as the morning star.[15] The symbol of the East, then, is one of rebirth and resurrection:

> C'est donc par excellence la région de la jeunesse, du jeune maïs, des jeunes dieux de la végétation, toujours peints et vêtus de rouge, du chant, des fêtes, de l'aurore. Pour les anciens Mexicains, toutes ces images s'identi-

fiaient avec une réalité géographique: la côte du Golfe,
la terre chaude de l'est, "au bord de la mer divine, de
l'eau celeste", selon l'expression des Annales de
Cuauhtitlán.[16]

[It is then the region par excellence of youth, young
corn, young gods of vegetation, always painted and
dressed in red, songs, festivals, and dawn. For the an-
cient Mexicans all these images were identified with a
geographic reality: the Gulf coast, the warm land of the
east, "along the divine sea, the celestial water," ac-
cording to the Annals of Cuauhtitlán.]

One would expect, then, that the first section would re-
flect the qualities of the East, and it does in several ways. The
setting is obviously paradisiacal. The complex development
of tree-water imagery (verses 1-3) and the ambiguity of the
identification (that is, whether the object is tree, fountain, or
both at the same time) evoke an ideal landscape, as does the
eternal river (4-6). The leisurely and timeless flow of water
(7-10) conveys a basic sense of harmony, particularly in
"unánime presencia en oleaje" [surging unanimous pres-
ence], that reaches its fullest development in line 12 and the
brilliant simile of opening wings in the center of the sky.

This implied landscape of the following stanza clearly is a
primitive forest, with the imagery reinforcing again the ele-
ments of nature: thickets, the bird whose singing petrifies the
woods, and happiness disappearing among the branches like
fruit on which birds feed. The next five stanzas are a hymn in
praise of the poet's beloved (23-75), in which physical charac-
teristics are converted into abstractions ("cuerpo de luz fil-
trada por un ágata" [body of light filtered through an agate];
"tu vientre es una playa soleada" [your abdomen is a sunny
beach]; "eres una ciudad que el mar asedia" [you are a city
besieged by the sea]) which become associated finally with a
rain goddess ("tu falda de maiz ondula y canta" [your corn
skirt ripples and sings]; "toda la noche llueves, todo el
día / abres mi pecho con tus dedos de agua" [all night you
rain, all day / you open my chest with your fingers of water]).

In the concluding stanza of this first hymn, the poet wanders through the corporeal geography that he has assembled from the abstractions, returning, through comparisons to river and woods, to the first landscape. Youth, growth, beginnings, dawn, vegetation, water—all are clearly attributes of the East associated with the inauguration of the poem.

With the stanza beginning at line 67, there is a transition that begins with a continuation of the praise of her body (67 and 68 echo verses 41, "voy por tu cuerpo"; 53, "voy por tus ojos"; and 56, "voy por tu frente") and a parallel continuation of nature imagery. But now, for the first time, nature becomes dangerous, "como por un sendero en la montaña / que en un abismo brusco se termina" [as if along a mountain path / that ends in an abrupt abyss]. The poet's shadow—in fact, his identity—is shattered, and he tries in vain to recover the fragments.

The following two stanzas dwell on the total dispersion of the poet's personality, a motif that acquires increasing importance as it reappears through the remainder of the work. Everything that the poet sees and touches, everything that he is, disintegrates totally. In this section, the poem's first subclimax is reached through the denial of time, recalling the riddle of the epigraph and revealing its connection with the poet's awareness of his lack of identity:

> piso días, instantes caminados,
> piso los pensamientos de mi sombra,
> piso mi sombra en busca de un instante,
> [95-97]

> [I tread days, moments that have been walked on,
> I tread the thoughts of my shadow
> I tread my shadow in search of a moment,]

Lines 98 and 99 continue the poet's search, but with more pleasant associations, appropriate to the description that follows of girls leaving school. In spite of the marked change of subject and tone, the new stanza still has time as its theme. The emergence of the girls—particularly the fact that they

come out of "su entraña rosada" [its pink womb]—suggests
birth. The temporarily unnamed girl is the center of a litany
in the lengthy stanza that follows, verses 109-41. The praise
rests on a series of occasionally paradoxical epithets that have
as a common denominator the magical things of life. She is,
in fact, a catalog of wondrous things, a composite of all
women:

> adolescente rostro innumerable,
> he olvidado tu nombre, Melusina,
> Laura, Isabel, Perséfona, María,
> tienes todos los rostros y ninguno,
> eres todas las horas y ninguna,
> te pareces al árbol y a la nube,
> eres todos los pájaros y un astro,
> te pareces al filo de la espada
> y a la copa de sangre del verdugo,
> yedra que avanza, envuelve y desarraiga
> al alma y la divide de sí misma,
> escritura de fuego sobre el jade,
> grieta en la roca, reina de serpientes,
>   [113-25]

> [adolescent multiple face,
> I have forgotten your name, Melusine,
> Laura, Isabel, Persephone, Mary,
> you have all faces and none,
> you are all hours and none,
> you are like the tree and the cloud,
> you are all birds and a star,
> you are like the sword edge
> and the bowl of blood of the executioner,
> ivy that advances, envelopes and dislodges
> the soul and divides it from itself,
> script of fire on jade,
> cleft in the rock, queen of serpents,]

The contrast here to the first part of the poem is attribut-
able in part to a change of geographical focus. Just as the East

was the dominant spirit of the introductory section, the subject matter here is influenced by the opposite directional point of Aztec cosmology. The West was known as Cuiatlampa, the place of women, and as the residence of goddesses and demigoddesses.[17] Pre-Columbian Mexicans prayed to the West for successful childbirth. The birth image, then, of the passage above, and even more the nameless girl who represents all women (including Melusine and Persephone), is a conscious choice of the poet to extend his theme in another direction of the calendar stone. This section ends, like the section on the East, with a return to the nameless, faceless, and timeless name, face, and moment (146-52). Parallel to the emptiness of the transition preceding this section is the transition to the next, still involved in time, even in its denial: "no hay nada frente a mí, sólo un instante" (153) [there is nothing facing me, only an instant].

The development in the first half of the poem of mythology associated with Aztec cardinal points is in effect a subtle link between the two halves, for the subject is clearly an extension of the poet's explanatory note. Aztec mythology, it might be argued, "belongs" to the second half. What should be noted, however, is that this mythology in the first half is not so much the subject as the setting, the background against which the development of the theme takes place. This incorporation of the second half is only the first of several carefully planned anticipations and echos.

After the development of the symbolisms of rebirth associated with the East and of femininity associated with the West, the reader logically seeks evidence of North and South, but it is not discernible. The reason may be found in Aztec mythology, which had not developed for these two points of the compass the clarity and strength that characterize the directions most closely connected with the appearance and disappearance of the central deity.

By bearing the main weight of the poem's meaning, the remaining pre-Columbian cardinal point, the center, compensates for the absence of North and South. In Aztec cosmology the center has a symbolic meaning that is lacking in the decorative compass rose of European geography:

C'est le lieu de croisement des autres directions, le lieu
de rencontre du haut et du bas. Les particularités des
espaces s'y totalisent. . . . Tantôt le centre est considéré
comme la synthese des autres espaces, participant de
leurs qualités diverses, et comme le lieu stable, où re-
pose le foyer divin de *Xiuhtecutli*, prototype et source de
tous les foyers; tantôt il n'est plus que le lieu inquiétant
des apparitions et des présages, le point de rencontre de
mondes étrangers. Il présente un aspect favorable et un
aspect néfaste, un aspect "droit" et un aspect
"gauche."[18]

[It is the crossroads of the other directions, the meeting
place of high and low. The special features of spaces are
added together there. . . . Sometimes the center is con-
sidered as the synthesis of the other spaces, participat-
ing in their different qualities, and as the static space, in
which there rests the divine hearth of *Xiuhtecutli*, the
prototype and source of all hearths; sometimes it is only
the disturbing place of apparitions and omens, the meet-
ing place of strange worlds. It presents a favorable and
unfavorable aspect, a "right" and a "left."]"

In addition to the line "Madrid, 1937" already indicated as
the numerical center of the poem, there is another center that
acquires its importance through regular recurrence. "Madrid,
1937" is in effect a linear division, both of the poet's life and of
his poem. The other, which we may call a symbolic center, is
recalled by the deliberate ambiguity of the epigraph, "C'est
toujours la seule." As the circular calendar rotates (or as the
eye reviews the stationary circles), a glyph that is apparently
the same appears, taking precedence over all others.

This symbolic center in the first half is characterized by
the reduction of the poet's consciousness to its simplest
element, the awareness of his own effort to understand. It is
preceded by a disintegration of the perception of the "real"
world, involving the surrealistic dismemberment of the poet
himself. This is the first of three subclimaxes in the first half
that represent the ultimate experience:

y a la salida de tu blanca frente
mi sombra despeñada se destroza,
recojo mis fragmentos uno a uno
y prosigo sin cuerpo, busco a tientas,
[72-75]
[and at the exit of your white brow
my fallen shadow is destroyed,
I pick up my fragments one by one
and go on, bodiless, searching and groping,]

Although it is defined in negative terms, the progressive
elimination of objective reality in an effort to define life's
essence, it is the first of three moments of transcendence in
the first half, for the poet has gone beyond himself to a new
awareness. These three moments together represent what
may be called construction through destruction.

It is significant that the first disintegration is situated
precisely between the sections symbolic of East and West.
The poet's experience preceding the first transcendence of
line 75 assumes the character of a quest, emphasized by the
constant repetition of "voy" [I go], which is obvious not only
at the beginning of stanzas in lines 34, 41, and twice, climac-
tically, in 67 and 68, but also as an explicit restatement
within stanzas (verses 37, 53, 56, and 58), always initiating
the verse. Although not as emphatic as "voy," the use of
"busco" [I seek], also always initiating a verse (85, 90, 98, 99)
suggests the continuation of the quest between the first and
second points of transcendence, a quest which is now defined
in terms of time: "busco una fecha viva como un pá-
jaro, / busco el sol de las cinco de la tarde" (98-99) [I seek a
living date like a bird, / I seek the sun at five in the after-
noon]. Between the second and third transcendences, a di-
gression on time interrupts the odyssey (171-88), which is
taken up dramatically as the poet is first led and then de-
stroyed by a feminine figure, leading into the nihilism of the
transcendence.

With verse 98 the goal is restated in positive terms. Time is
then lost sight of through the abstractions of feminine

qualities, culminating in a lengthy series of elaborate para-
doxes, until the second transcendence is reached in the
stanza headed by line 142. Here, at the midpoint of the first
half, the quarter point of the entire poem, is a climactic
development of the theme of time that fuses its positive
aspects, the goal of the search, with the negative, the impos-
sibility of its achievement. All of time is one single moment,
if only the poet could find it, capture it, and express it. Paz's
expression of the vitality of the present is indicated here, as in
other poems, by the use of "arde" (146) [burns] to symbolize
the essence of life rather than of destruction.

The section on the West, essentially a listing of miraculous
and sometimes paradoxical attributes that characterize both
a feminine divinity and a divine femininity, terminates with
a brief but powerful reflection of the circularity of time,
stressed by parallel repetition, especially in verses 148-50,
culminating again in the poet's existential awareness of him-
self.

The pessimism, nihilism, and desolate self-awareness of
the stanza beginning with line 153 echo exactly the tone of
the stanza headed by line 90, yet its full impact derives from
the restatement, so that its uniqueness—again a paradox—
rests on its repetition. The second experience gains from the
first, which on rereading gains from its anticipation of the
second. In this way time's circularity is expressed by the
poet's experience, by what he says about experience, and by
what the poem implies about both as an absolute.

Once again the awareness of time's circularity is accom-
panied by physical disintegration (165-70) and once again the
poet passes through to the other side in a stanza that is a
magic transition, both in form and theme (171-88). Time
again is the common denominator, but now the tone is joyous
and the imagery is fruitful. In a surrealistic sequence the
moment of time is both a seed and a ripening fruit, which
grows into a tree that is at the same time the poet. When the
circularity of time is invoked at the end of this passage,
therefore, a positive—or at least objective—attitude replaces
the previous bitterness.

Time's circularity resumes, after the stanza break of
194-95, with further development of its corrosive features.
Here the unidentified woman addressed (is she the same?)
seems to portray the opposite characteristics of the sensual
vision of verse 41:

> ardo sin consumirme, busco el agua
> y en tus ojos no hay agua, son de piedra,
> y tus pechos, tu vientre, tus caderas
> son de piedra, tu boca sabe a polvo,
> tu boca sabe a tiempo emponzoñado,
> tu cuerpo sabe a pozo sin salida,
> [200-205]

> [I burn without being consumed, I look for water
> and in your eyes there is no water, they are of stone,
> and your breasts, your belly, your hips
> are of stone, your mouth tastes of dust,
> your mouth tastes of poisoned time,
> your body tastes like a blocked well,]

Instead of being a rescuer from time's forces, she is now the
instrument of time's punishment. Through her comes the
disintegration that is the last subclimax of the poem's first
half:

> y tus palabras afiladas cavan
> mi pecho y me despueblan y vacían,
> uno a uno me arrancas los recuerdos,
> he olvidado mi nombre, mis amigos
> gruñen entre los cerdos o se pudren
> comidos por el sol en un barranco,
> [217-22]

> [and your sharpened words dig out
> my chest and desolate and empty me,
> one by one you tear out my memories,
> I have forgotten my name, my friends
> grunt among the pigs or rot
> devoured by the sun in a ravine,]

The result, once again, the only definable reality, is the poet's awareness of his own awareness:

conciencia traspasada por un ojo
que se mira mirarse hasta anegarse
de claridad:
                            [228-30]
[awareness pierced by an eye
which sees itself looking at itself until it is annihilated
in clarity:]

After each disintegration, the poet begins again. Or, rather, the poem continues to flow. In each case, the resumption begins with the immediate cause of the disintegration. In the first, the poet's search; in the second, time itself; in the third, the abstraction of woman. The parallel nature of these episodes is reinforced by the regularity of their spacing within the poem—approximately every seventy-five lines. Clearly their recurrence reinforces the poem's theme of circular time.

The last thirty lines of the first half, in their autobiographical references, concrete reminiscences, and lack of hermeticism, anticipate the dominant features of the second half. They are introduced, however, by a section terminating in questions of identity (260-61) and are followed by a dramatic confusion of terms designed to illustrate those questions (282-87). They thus represent a bridge to the second half, an extension of the philosophic questioning of the nature of time that is the poem's theme. The nihilism of each subclimax of transcendence is a denial of the intervening material, so that the questioning, although it seems to be the same, has a deepening, intensive, and cumulative effect. Each statement of circularity is a reminder to the reader of the previous subclimaxes. These are, both literally and figuratively, "instantes caminados" [traveled moments]. The conclusion of the first half suggests that the poet has not gone anywhere in his quest, for he continues to be the prisoner of his awareness, which is the only instrument he can use to defeat time.

In the second half, the direction of the poet's experience is outward rather than inward. Here the experience of love is dominant, and it is not "yo" but "tu y yo" that is the essence. Love is the mystical approach to life in this half, and becomes its goal, so that the tone, contrasting with the first half, is optimistic. The three subclimaxes of the first half have a counterpart in the four subclimaxes of the second. What both halves share is the recurring transcendence—or attempted transcendence—of time and reality. This is the regular appearance of the symbolic center that unites the structure of the entire poem.

The second half of the poem constitutes a most dramatic change simply by changing its setting to the exterior world and making society, rather than the individual psyche, its main subject. This change is further intensified by the violence of the bombardment of Madrid, in the midst of which a couple seeks security and peace by making love. Whether through the objectivity of "vuelven al principio" or the subjectivity of the exclamation "oh ser total," or the skillful transition from third-person description to first-person-plural participation of verses 295-97, a process of integration is suggested that is the diametrical opposite of the poet's previous disintegration:

> los dos se desnudaron y se amaron
> por defender nuestra porción eterna,
> nuestra ración de tiempo y paraíso,
> tocar nuestra raíz y recobrarnos,
> recobrar nuestra herencia arrebatada
> por ladrones de vida hace mil siglos,
> los dos se desnudaron y besaron
> porque las desnudeces enlazadas
> saltan el tiempo y son invulnerables,
> nada las toca, vuelven al principio,
> no hay tú ni yo, mañana, ayer ni nombres,
> verdad de dos en solo un cuerpo y alma,
> oh ser total. . .
> [295-307]

[the two undressed and made love
to defend our eternal allocation,
our allocation of time and paradise,
to touch our root and recover ourselves,
to recover our inheritance snatched
by the thieves of life a thousand centuries ago,
the two undressed and kissed each other
because entwined naked bodies
leap over time and are invulnerable,
nothing touches them, they return to the beginning,
there is no you or I, tomorrow, yesterday or names,
the truth of two in a single body and soul,
oh total being . . .]

The following stanza appears to turn its back on the lovers
by taking a broad view of society as seen in various rooms and
individuals that are generalized finally through a series of
disconnected abstractions, which are in turn transformed
into space (321-28). Here, as in every subclimax of the poem,
time is involved in the transformation, but now linear time is
defeated by love:

no hay tiempo ya, ni muro: ¡espacio, espacio,
abre la mano, coge esta riqueza,
corta los frutos, come de la vida,
tiéndete al pie del árbol, bebe el agua!,
                                                        [330-33]

[there is no longer any time, or wall: space, space,
open your hand, pick this richness,
cut the fruit, eat of life,
stretch out below the tree, drink the water!]

Love, to be sure, is only implied in the lines just cited, but
its implication originates in the timeless union, the paradise
regained, of verse 305. Furthermore, the statement of love's
triumph is immediately restated explicitly in the opening
lines of the following stanza:

    todo se transfigura y es sagrado,
    es el centro del mundo cada cuarto,
    es la primera noche, el primer día,
    el mundo nace cuando dos se besan,
                [334-37]

    [everything is transfigured and is sacred,
    each room is the center of the world,
    it is the first night, the first day,
    when two people kiss, the world is born,]

With no transition now, the focus is again social, with a gallery of caricatures of professions and types. In fact, there is a progression of the nontranscendent material from concreteness to generality, from description to increasing abstraction. After the catalog of unpleasantness that fills twenty verses, all dependent on the final verb "se derrumban," it is love, in the third transcendence of this half, that provides the vision of peace, unity, and fullness of life:

                se derrumban
    por un instante inmenso y vislumbramos
    nuestra unidad perdida, el desamparo
    que es ser hombres, la gloria que es ser hombres
    y compartir el pan, el sol, la muerte,
    el olvidado asombro de estar vivos;
                       [359-64]

            [are demolished
    for an immense instant and we glimpse
    our lost unity, the vulnerability
    of being men, the glory of being men
    and sharing bread, the sun, death,
    the forgotten amazement of being alive;]

This idea is developed in verses 365-76, and summarized in the last two lines of that section: "el mundo cambia / si dos se miran y se reconocen, / amar es desnudarse de los nombres:" [the world changes / if two look at and recognize each other, / loving is stripping one's names:].

The series of images of ugliness that follows is parallel to lines 340-60 in the contrast provided between ideal and real worlds. The poet gives a list of sins, a select list of crimes against the social order (suicide, incest, murder, adultery, sodomy) that are preferable to the tedium of time. Repugnant though they are, they are better than the monotony, emptiness, and bonds of linear time, characterized as "mierda abstracta."

After a brief, puzzling, and unexpected view of God, not attained through love, the poet resumes the quest. The novelty of the stanza headed by verse 408 lies in its return to the elements of the poem's first half: "sigo mi desvarío" [I continue my delirium], "camino a tientas por los corredores / del tiempo" [I grope through the corridors / of time], "vuelvo adonde empecé" [I return where I began], "camino por las calles de mí mismo" [I walk through the streets of myself]. But a feminine "tú" annihilates solitude, and once again the tension is resolved through the happy union of the lovers, the abolition of time, the ultimate reality without names, and the real perception of time, "tiempo total donde no pasa nada / sino su propio transcurrir dichoso" (424-34) [total time where nothing happens / but its own happy passing].

If one looks back at the scenes of ecstasy that stop time for the poet and give a new dimension to reality, one sees a pattern of regularity: 301-10, 329-37, 359-80, and 424-34 are sections approximately thirty verses apart for the first three, with a double gap of approximately sixty between the third and fourth. These parallel in regularity those we observed in the first part, which contains three peaks of transcendence approximately seventy-five lines apart: 75-97, 152-70, 217-30. These transcendent experiences are alike in their objective—the annihilation of individual personality—but diametrically opposed in character. Those in the first half, characterized by the epigraph from "Artémis," turn inward, exploring and distilling the experience of solitude in time until nothing is left but the awareness of awareness. Those in the second half, under the benign influence of Venus, achieve victory over time through love. Essentially, these are opposite sides of the same coin. In both halves, the timeless area is the center of the poem to which the theme regularly returns. In the Aztec calendar, the center, we recall, is the fifth cardinal point of the compass. In the poem, it takes precedence over the others.

The long section of verses 435-87 is nothing less than a disquisition on history, which leads to questions about its meaning. The answers, and particularly verse 490 ("no hay redención, no vuelve atrás el tiempo" [there is no redemption, time does not turn back]), are a deliberately monotonous recall of the first half, already recalled in the second by verses 392-94. The governing thought of this stanza is verse 498: "cada minuto es nada para siempre" [each minute is nothing forever].

That the poet has reached a philosophical dead end in his search is apparent in his abandonment of the direct treatment of time in the concluding portion of the poem. He transfers his anguish instead to a related area, the meaning of life in general and the individual's place in it. The prayer of the conclusion (beginning with verse 533) is anticipated in the summoning of Eloise, Persephone, and Mary (history, mythology, and Christianity) to reveal their true identities so that the poet will know his.

Presumably addressed to a pre-Columbian deity, the prayer is, in its urgency, the most moving section of the work. The anguish of the litany stems from the hope of the poet's (and mankind's) release from the narrow limits of time. The prayer is granted (574-83) and the poet enters a paradise, constructed of the intricate water imagery of the poem's last six lines. With the description of the river that is both source and terminus, the poem concludes characteristically and boldly with an adverb and a colon that promise infinity: "y llega siempre:" [and always arrives:].

The colon symbolizes the circular structure of the poem by creating the expectation of continuation. If the reader is not aware at first reading that lines 585-90 are repetitions of the first six verses, the colon dramatically returns him to the introduction.[19] The only possible continuation, therefore, is that of the text previously read. The actual conclusion, indicated by Paz's note, ought to be verse 584 ("y su magia de espejos revivía" [and revived its mirror magic]), which suggests the illusory qualities of life associated with the poet's previous use of the mirror. Syntactically, however, verse 584 cannot be a conclusion, for the objects of the verb are stated only in the verses that follow it. The reader is necessarily led on to the lines beyond, which are both concluding and introductory.

The closing of the poem's cycle with verse 584, the synodic course of Venus, recalls the connection with the calendar system. In particular, one should think of the five days at the end of the solar year, which do not fit into a regular unit and yet somehow must be counted before a new year can begin. Perhaps because their system was otherwise so symmetrically and intricately arranged, the Aztecs dreaded as ominous these odd days, called *nemontemi*, the nameless or unfortunate days. Although the five verses 585-90 need not be regarded as ominous, they may be; in any case, their vital function outside of the formal line count draws an exact analogy with the *nemontemi*.

The fear that the world would end was not limited to the *nemontemi*. It is also apparent at both extremes of the Aztec calendar, the days and the eras. The daily course of the sun, far from being taken for granted, was viewed as a minor miracle that required man's constant cooperation, for the sun depended on the sustenance that could be provided only with sacrificial blood, preferably human. At the other extreme of time's scale was the conclusion of an era, when the fate, not only of the world, but of the universe, hung in the balance. In Aztec mythology, the world had been destroyed and recreated four times. The entire Aztec cosmology, therefore, was not only elaborately cyclical, but fragile, for the circular movement could be halted at any juncture. Any moment of ending and beginning, of which the concluding verses here are a symbol, is regarded with awe, and, finally, with exultation,

which culminates in exaltation of the forces that cause re-
newal.

Although the entire Aztec calendar is composed of inter-
locking cycles, the deity who is most specifically charged
with the process of renewal after destruction is Quetzalcoatl,
probably the newest, youngest, and most dominant god in
terms of popularity. Temples dedicated to him are always
circular. His calendar sign is 4 *Ehécatl* [wind], and he is
frequently depicted wearing the mask of Ehécatl, whose tem-
ples are also round. In his hand Quetzalcoatl carries the wind
jewel, a round section of conch shell with five segments.

The use of Aztec myth at the poem's conclusion to sym-
bolize destruction and renewal fuses, appropriately, with the
intention of the epigraph, and suggests that the two, like the
two halves which each dominates, are both separate and
identical. The first half analyzes time and reality through a
process of disintegration; the second aspires to the same
objective through the opposite process of integration and
synthesis. These are, therefore, opposite sides of the same
reality. The conclusion, which applies to both, is that the
discernible meaning, whether negative or positive, must be
derived from the process of circularity.

The second principal effect of merging the poem's con-
clusion with its introduction is to suggest the possibility—or
rather, the obligation—of multiple readings and interpreta-
tions. In the same way that the climaxes of transcendence in
each half are both separate and cumulative, so the reading of
the entire poem gains from previous readings. The process of
disintegration of the first half can be seen in subsequent
readings to be balanced by the creative, social, and optimistic
synthesis of the second half; the latter can be seen as only a
prelude to the inevitable corrosion and nihilism so elo-
quently depicted in the first half. Even more, the circularity
of structure leads to a loss of direction. Which is the "first"
half? The poem becomes quite different in tone if the halves
are reversed. Indeed the division into halves does not nec-
essarily suggest an appropriate point of beginning. The ul-
timate effect of circularity ought to be to suggest that

the poem—if we ignore the epigraph—could begin with any verse. In this way Paz explored in structure the method that he was to use later in the more complicated technique of *Blanco*, in which he broadened multiple interpretation through "modular" themes.

3 *Salamandra*
The Subject Itself

decir es mondadura

[Speaking is pruning]
—Paz, "Solo a dos voces"

In contrast to the circular pattern of *Piedra de sol* and to the alternations of communion and solitude, light and darkness, optimism and pessimism that are the spokes of the circle, *Salamandra* represents a different approach to the reader. In judging this book, the reader's main problem is the identification of the pattern. In fact, his first impression may be that the book has little unity and that it simply presents a variety of poems, largely unpunctuated, that continue the techniques of *Libertad bajo palabra* and *La estación violenta.* That they do so is undeniable. What is different, as we shall see in the poems analyzed in this chapter, is the concentration on the subject as a means of forcing the reader to study both the theme and his own reaction to it.

With the exception of several reviews, one of the few significant commentaries on *Salamandra*'s position in its writer's development is expressed by Xirau. His brief but illuminating commentary defines the book as a transition that is at the same time a stylistic departure from the previous work and a foreshadowing of further innovation in *Blanco.* The change of technique is so obvious that it is disorienting. Yet the break with Paz's previous development suggests change rather than discontinuity. The devices that Xirau defines—alternating elements, complementary readings, and increased reliance on paradox—are seen as new expressions of the poet's underlying philosophy of art and life.[1]

Two other devices in *Salamandra* that mark a broadening of Paz's techniques to intensify the involvement of the reader are columnar typography and the omission of punctuation. The latter was initiated in 1950-54 in some of the poems of *Semillas para un himno*, which utilize capital letters but omit commas and periods. In *Piedra de sol* the poet varied his procedure by omitting capital letters and periods, relying only on commas. In many of the poems of *Salamandra* he reverts to the earlier form. Clearly he is working toward a flexibility in punctuation which requires that the reader supply a variety of pauses according to his personal response to the text.

A similar experimentation for the same purpose is evident in columnar structure, that is, initiating verses in the center or on the right-hand side of the page instead of at the left margin. This technique, also already used in some of the poems of *Semillas para un himno*, emphasizes the circular structure of *Piedra de sol*, and reappears in *Salamandra*. Like the omission of punctuation, it suggests the reception of the text as variable rather than rigid. The reader is encouraged to perceive that multiple voices and tones exist. The pattern of beginning verses at the right side of the page or in the center frequently assumes the dimension of an echo or a different speaker, and sometimes is in oppsition to the verses initiated on the left. These effects, however, are not fully developed until the composition of *Ladera este*. It is interesting to note that they begin with the poems dated 1950-54 and that they increase in number and complexity as Paz deepens his interest in the reader's response to, and participation in, the text.

The expressiveness of "Repeticiones" is attributable to the ways in which its structure and rhythm reinforce its theme. Its anguish, as implied by the title, has no source. Its point of departure is, to use the phrase of Borges' "El milagro secreto," "mero terror" [mere terror]. The contradiction opens up a series of gradations that constitute a closed circle of suffering.

The first seven verses, which provide the initial definition of anxiety, stand out from the rest of the poem for their brevity:

El corazón y su redoble iracundo

el obscuro caballo de la sangre
cáballo ciego caballo desbocado
el carrousel nocturno la noria del terror
el grito contra el muro y la centella rota
Camino andado
    camino desandado

[The heart and its wrathful beating
the dark horse of blood
blind horse runaway horse
the nocturnal carrousel the treadmill of terror
the cry against the wall and the broken flash
Road traveled
    road untraveled]

Although there are no stanzas here, the refrain of "Camino andado / camino desandado" divides the remainder of the poem into approximately equal parts. The more impersonal the description is, particularly in the absence of verbs and pronouns ("el corazón", "la sangre", "el grito"), the more personal is its application to the poet. The subject, the frightened beating of his heart, is stressed by the rhythm of the first four verses, which captures the sound of the beating heart like a stethoscope. Verses 3-5 consist of two metaphors each, paralleling in subject and sound the "corazón y su redoble" of the first verse. The third verse, "caballo ciego caballo desbocado," is intensely onomatopoetic. This introductory section defines the poem's subject by establishing the approach and by setting the tone. The refrain, with its echoes of the heartbeat, effectively repeats the underlying rhythm.

The second section is a detailed explanation of verse 4, with repetitions that graphically portray the circularity of the "carrousel nocturno," a metaphor which becomes increasingly ironic. Although verbs create an impression of action here, their use is limited to verses 9-10 and is subordinated in adjectival clauses that modify the noun "la pena," which initiates these two verses and the following. More important is the use of these verbs to portray a personal connection lacking in the introductory section: "la pena que

interrogo cada día" [the suffering that I question each day]
and "la pena que no se aparta y cada noche me despierta" [the
suffering that will not leave and that awakens me each night].
These personal verbs dramatize the abstractions in the same
section, lending force to "El cuerpo a cuerpo con un pensa-
miento afilado" [Hand to hand combat with a sharpened
thought] and "el alfiler y el párpado traspasado" [the pin and
the pierced eyelid], so that it is the "yo" of "interrogo" who
struggles and is pierced. In the same way the other abstrac-
tions of the section are personalized and thus perceived more
clearly by the reader who identifies with the poet's anguish.
Paz uses violence to convey the nature of the struggle in
verses 12-15. Although they represent an amplification of
verse 8, they are more graphic and more painful in their
imagery than the abstract symbolism of the earlier line. The
pain of the pierced eyelid is universalized by making it the
symbol of the badly lived day. That symbol is reinforced by
the four metaphors that immediately follow and amplify it,
four mini-dramas suggested by "manchada" [stained],
"escupida" [spat on], "loca" [crazy], and "puta" [whore]. The
violence of the four taken together contrasts with the two
nonviolent abstractions that frame them in verses 11 and 16.
    The first verse of the third section, whose first reference is
"El coso de la sangre" [The enclosure of the blood], echoes the
sound of the refrain that immediately precedes it, and the
assonance of "pica" and "rechifla" adds another echo. As the
catalog of distress continues, the third section intensifies
feeling through concreteness of imagery. In portraying the
abstractions of suffering, whose cause remains unknown
throughout the poem, the imagery relies on vivid detail. The
use of "y" divides 22 and 25-27 into two approximately equal
parts that repeat the double beat of the refrain. The violence
of the second section is followed by the corrosion and
obstruction of the third, expressed in terms of stagnation,
acidity, rust, gangrene, and a gag. As a summary of this
section, following the graphic details, verse 27 gains in
strength what it lacks in detail.
    The fourth section returns to the accumulation of detail,

whose negative qualities are less graphic than those of the preceding stanzas. Verse 30 ("El vaso de agua la pastilla la lengua de estaño" [The glass of water the pill the tongue of tin]), for example, reflects the discouragement of every sick person who has no faith in medication. The blood, the night, and the nothingness of verses 32-34 are not strongly disturbing in themselves. What makes them so is the dreamlike context of the surrealistic images of verses 37-49. These verses and the more innocuous preceding section (verses 30-36) are stressed by the strongly rhythmic repetitions and internal rhymes of "cascada negra de la sangre / cascada pétrea de la noche" [black waterfall of blood / stony waterfall of night] and of "aparición del ojo y el muro que gesticula / aparición del metro cojo / el puente roto y el ahogado" [appearance of the eye and the gesticulating wall / appearance of the limping meter / the broken bridge and the drowned man].

The heartbeat rhythms, alternating double with triple beats, dominate the entire final section:

> El pensamiento circular y el círculo de familia
> ¿qué hice qué hiciste qué hemos hecho?
> el laberinto de la culpa sin culpa
> el espejo que acusa y el silencio que se gangrena
> el día estéril la noche estéril el dolor estéril
> la soledad promiscua el mundo despoblado
> la sala de espera en donde ya no hay nadie
> Camino andado y desandado
> la vida se ha ido sin volver el rostro

> [Circular thought and the family circle
> what did I do what did you do what have we done?
> the labyrinth of guilt without guilt
> the accusing mirror and gangrenous silence
> sterile day sterile night sterile pain
> promiscuous solitude deserted world
> the waiting room in which there is no one
> Road traveled and untraveled
> life has gone away without turning its face]

The circle of verse 42 symbolizes hopelessness, as do unfounded guilt, introspection, and anguished silence. In verses 47-48, the poet's suffering becomes universal, so that there is no longer hope for anyone. The climax of the poem is constructed not by repeating the refrain at the end, as a more traditional technique might, but by using it as the penultimate verse. The emphasis thus falls on the final verse, which is rather flat in tone and rhythm when taken out of context. In the final position, however, it is remarkably forceful. Furthermore, except for the verbs of verse 43, which are parenthetical in context, the final verse stands out as the only independent action of the entire poem.

Perhaps only in the reading of the final verse does the reader become fully aware of the absence of independent verbs in the preceding 49 verses. That absence, stressed by the persistent listing of nouns (which initiate all the verses except 21, 36, and 43), reduces the complexities of life to a catalog of items whose relationship to each other is established by the tone of the poem. Furthermore, the solitary and climactic position of the final verse lends strength to a flat intransitive verb. It also marks a change in direction by interrupting, if not terminating, the circularity suggested by the refrain.

The final verse dominates the poem by summarizing the theme, in which we can see additional evidence of the transcendence of the circularity of *Piedra de sol.* The outstanding characteristic of life, as it eludes the grasp of the poet, is the impersonality of its personification, in contrast to the keenly felt anguish of the rest of the poem. By reducing all of his existence to life without a face, representing a question without an answer, the poet obligates the reader to pose the same question to himself. Whatever the reply may be, it lies outside the text of the poem. The theme has been reduced to the essence not of the poet's response but the reader's.

"Aquí" displays the same correspondence between theme and form, although much more succinctly. In its eight verses (which, since the single words of verses 2 and 4 belong metrically to the subsequent verses, are really six) the poet travels a full metaphysical circle:

                    Aquí
        Mis pasos en esta calle
        Resuenan
                    en otra calle
        donde
            oigo mis pasos
        pasar en esta calle
        donde
        Sólo es real la niebla

            [Here
        My steps in this street
        Resound
                    in another street
        where
            I hear my steps
        go by in this street
        where

        Only the mist is real]

The first verse, read alone, expresses a clarity that is di-
ametrically opposed to the mist of the final verse. The fact
that these steps are echoed in another street is stressed by the
broken typography of the following verse, so that both
"resuenan" and "en otra calle" are strengthened by the posi-
tion of the words. A similar effect of logical simplicity, step by
step, is conveyed by the next two verses. Here, in the center of
the poem, reality is split, for the reader—and the poet—
assumes that "mis pasos" of verse 5 are the same as those of
the first verse, and that he has in fact returned to the original
street. The mystery is that "otra calle" and "esta calle" are
simultaneously identical and different, and that the steps
(and therefore the poet) must participate in the same duality.
The unpunctuated form and the statement of the last verse,
which is open rather than final in its meaning, suggest para-
doxically that movement and uncertainty are the only cer-
tainties.

    The parallelism of "calle" in 1, 3, and 6, and the repetitions
of "donde" and "mis pasos" indicate formally the repetitions

of sound, identity, and place conveyed by the meaning. The final "donde," a hanging bridge that crosses a chasm whose other side is not visible, is particularly effective. Like "Repeticiones," this poem transcends circularity in its final verse, and presents a paradox to the reader. If only mist is real, is there any reality outside the poem?

"La palabra escrita," an example of Paz's use of the poetic process as his subject, is a return to circularity. In writing this poem, he attempts to capture concretely the elusive and magical nature of writing by examining himself in the acts of observing and recording. The poem is written in two voices, one conscious and another, in long parenthetical sections, that is, if not subconscious, at least an inner voice. Yet on closer examination, the conscious voice is seen as a refrain ("Ya escrita la primera / palabra [Already written the first / word] beyond which the poet cannot pass. It is, therefore, a barrier to his writing of the poem that it initiates. At the same time, it divides the poem into sections that function as stanzas. The first three sections are equal in length (five verses each); the last three have six, seven, and three verses.

Since the conscious voice is a short refrain, it requires no punctuation. Its use of the capital letter indicates that the poet makes a fresh start by returning to the words he has written. The inner voice of the parentheses, however, always begins with a small letter and is fully punctuated with commas. The period is omitted, but its absence, because of the parentheses, is not felt strongly until the last verse.

The first parenthetical phrase is a contradiction of the word that the poet has just written, a contradiction at three levels: (1) the word is different from the poet's intention; (2) it contradicts his intention; (3) it is closer to the intention by not stating it. The last paradox implies a meaning beyond the limits of language.

The second section begins with a count (of words passing in review, or of the passage of time, or both?) that ends with three and then lists the subjects of the action that is to be developed in the following sections: "uno, dos, tres / arriba el sol, tu cara / en el centro del pozo, / fija como un sol atónito" [one, two, three / the sun above, your face / in the center of the well, / fixed like an astonished sun]. The metaphor of the face reflected in the well not only immobilizes the face but also personalizes the sun.

After the introduction, in the second section, of the main elements—the personae—of the dramatized metaphor, the action follows in three "scenes." The third section (verse 11) continues the counting of the second and presents the beginning of the implied narrative that will develop in slow motion through the fourth and fifth sections. The central action of the poem, the fall of a pebble into the well where a face is reflected, is amplified by the details of the face's expressions, the trajectory of the pebble, and the reflected sun. In the third section the action begins *in medias res* as the falling stone is observed first, continues with the expression of the face contemplating the fall, and ends with the imagined reaction of the observer (not necessarily the poet), who, by counting the seconds of the fall, links this section with the preceding and with the fifth.

The concept of time, the vivid use of the present tense to slow down a rapid action by describing its components, unites the fourth section with the preceding one. Here, however, the face in the well and the stone acquire second meanings, as both "otra" of verse 17 and "la que" of verses 18 and 19 refer to "palabra." It is the reflected face, waiting for the projectile, that is "la palabra / antes de la caída y de la cuenta" [the word / before the fall and the count]. The abyss represents the emptiness before creation, out of which the word, poetry, creates meaning.

The fifth section stands out for its change of tense, stressed by the quadruple use of "verás" [you will see] to initiate verses 24-27. It portrays not so much a slowing down as a stopping of the action (indicated by the recount from two to four) while the poet imagines its consequences. The reflected images will be shattered and yet the same. This collision of action with immobility, of the temporary with the permanent, and of fragmentation with unity, represents the essence of poetic creativity. The essence of meaning is transitory.

The final brief section is the poet's ironic commentary on his success and his failure. It is, at the same time, an incomplete conclusion, indicated by the omission of the period, which keeps the poem open. Yet it is also a philosophical definition of reality. If all that matters is the counting of the words (that is, "no hay más palabras que las de la cuenta," the recapitulation), it is the process rather than its objective that is the ultimate reality.

The progress of the poem, therefore, rests not on action but on the changing perceptions that both the reader and the poet have of the initial statement, the writing of the first word. Although in a superficial sense the poem has not advanced at all, its structure consists of the reduction of the poet's thought to its essence, which is the clear vision of a fragment of reality before it is obscured by its expression in language. In this way Paz involves the reader in his mission of simplifying experience.

Like *Pasado en claro*, which it anticipates in several ways, "Noche en claro" is ambiguous in its title. In one meaning the poet refers to an all-night vigil. In another he refers to his evaluation of that experience, the night seen clearly. The poem's significance for the present study lies not so much in either interpretation as in the awareness that the events and meaning of the night are not necessarily clear, much less unified. In that sense the title can be interpreted ironically, particularly if the reader has more than one interpretation of the experience.

The first stanza rests on a solid base of realistic and autobiographical detail as the poet recalls his meeting with two friends (perhaps André Breton and Benjamin Péret, to whom the poem is dedicated) in a Paris café. Although autumn is characterized by several abstract and surrealistic metaphors, the rest of this stanza consists of objective description of the scene, concluding with verses which become a refrain in their use at the end of the second and fourth stanzas: "Algo se prepara" [Something is being prepared]. The initial subject, then, is the poet's promise and the reader's expectation.

The promise is intensified in the second stanza: time divides; not only do the dead live, but the living are truly

alive; and the city itself "se abre como un corazón, como un higo la flor que es fruto" [opens like a heart, like a fig the flower that is fruit]. If it were not for the stanza's concluding reference to something imminent, the reader would feel that he was participating in one of Paz's ecstatic moments of fulfillment, like those in *Piedra de sol* and "Himno entre ruinas."
The change of subject and tone in the third stanza is so abrupt that the reader is stunned. With the exception of the link provided by the reference to autumn, there is no transition from the first two stanzas. The description of the London subway is expressed in negative terms and destructive imagery, particularly faceless, bloodless, nameless people, and meaningless time in its circular motion. Against this background appears an adolescent couple in love, evidenced not only in their posture but in the four letters linked on the young man's fingers which, in the final verse of the stanza ("mano que das el sueño y das la resurrección" [your hand that gives sleep and that gives resurrection], symbolize the nonreligious redemption of man.
The principal problem in comprehending the poem thus far consists in reconciling its parts and in defining its theme. At the beginning of the fourth stanza, precisely in the middle of the poem's 141 verses, is the guidance that other poems might ordinarily provide in the conclusion:

> Todo es puerta
>   todo es puente
> ahora marchamos en la otra orilla
> mira abajo correr el río de los siglos
> el río de los signos
> Mira correr el río de los astros

> [Everything is a door
>   everything is a bridge
> now we are going along on the other shore
> look at the river of the centuries flow below
> the river of signs
> Look at the river of the stars flow]

The answer to the question of theme is provided in part by the point of view, which is that of infinity. *Sub specie aeternitatis*, the world and its inhabitants are reduced to insignificance. Along with them, the poem—at least the first three stanzas—has lost its substance. The fourth stanza is a series of abstractions that vaporize the reality with which the poem began. All that remains is the sound of the poem's words ("sílabas que alguien dice / palabras que alguien oye" [syllables that someone says / words that someone hears]) and the feeling, now stated for the last time, that something is imminent.

The fifth stanza continues the subject and tone of the first as the poet takes leave of his friends and autumn resumes its march. The destructive nature of time, continuing the tone of the third stanza, is also resumed. The stanza concludes with a paradox that stresses the permanence of poetry.

The length of the sixth stanza, like that of the second, marks a complete change in the poem's direction. Here the subject is "Ciudad o Mujer Presencia" [City or Woman Presence], in which the poet's perception of the city is expressed in predominantly erotic imagery:

Pero tu sexo es innombrable
la otra cara del ser
la otra cara del tiempo
el revés de la vida
Aquí cesa todo discurso
aquí la belleza no es legible
aquí la presencia se vuelve terrible
replegada en sí misma la Presencia es vacío
lo visible es invisible
Aquí se hace visible lo invisible

[But your sex is unnameable
the other face of being
the other face of time
the reverse of life
Here all discourse ceases
here beauty is not legible

here the presence becomes terrible
folded in itself the Presence is emptiness
the visible is invisible
Here the invisible becomes visible]

Through eroticism the poet reaches the point where op-
posites merge, where time stops, and where the points of the
compass join. Paz's readers are familiar with the mood if not
the precise geography, for this is the essence of life, feeling,
and being whose definition is the object of so much of his
poetry. What is surprising is its presence in this poem, which
now has the effect of a collage. That effect is only intensified
by the final stanza, an epilogue of three verses.

This structure (or, rather, lack of structure) represents the
poet's attempt to involve the reader's feelings in the inter-
pretation of the poem. If the reader remains outside the poem,
he will see only its lack of unity and may react in negative
ways to what seems to be a lack of theme. Yet the "desubstan-
tiation" of the subject is in effect the theme, or at least part of
it. To the extent that the reader can identify with and dupli-
cate the poet's experience during that night in Paris, he will
feel its meaning, even though he may not be able to articulate
his feelings. This essentially was the poet's problem, which
led to his expression of an incomplete poem. Paz's process
consists in transferring to the reader the responsibility not
only for completing the poem, but even for defining its
theme.

The textual revisions of "Noche en claro," although few in
number, significantly aid the reader in the comprehension of
the poem. If we compare the first edition (1962) with that of
Poemas (1979), the most obvious change is the division into
seven stanzas. By using separation that suggests structure, if
not narrative, in a poem that is lacking the latter, Paz invites
the reader to search for, participate in, or create a pattern of
organization.

The omission of several verses of the first edition in the
first stanza of the 1979 version can be viewed as simplifica-
tion. The first of these, "Algo se prepara / Dijo uno de

nosotros" (*Salamandra*, 59, lines 11-12) [Something is being prepared / Said one of us], not only anticipates the climax of the 1979 stanza, but weakens it when the verses are repeated. The effective use of "Algo se prepara," with variations, as a refrain is strengthened by avoiding repetition and using it dramatically only at the conclusion of stanzas.

The deletion of "Piedras chorreando tiempo / Casas inválidas ateridos osarios / Oh huesos todavía con fiebre" (*Salamandra*, 59, lines 15-17) [Stones dripping time / Invalid houses frozen boneyards / Oh still feverish bones] from the first stanza of the 1979 text unifies the concrete description of the street scene. The abstract symbols of these verses represent in the first version a personal symbolism that intrudes on the depiction of the deserted street and its effect on the poet's state of mind. The third of the deleted verses is appropriately added to the second stanza, where it follows and strengthens the image of resurrection (*Poemas*, 350, lines 2-3). In the same way, "Se abre de par en par la vida" [life opens wide] of the first version is deleted because it is out of place in anticipating the ecstatic vision that is the subject of the second stanza in the revision.

The omission of "Nada se dice excepto lo indecible" (*Salamandra*, 60, line 14) [Nothing is said except the unsayable] is a result of the creation of stanzas in the later version. That verse, which logically follows the refrain, has no connection with the line that follows in the first version, "Este mismo año vacilante" [this same vacillating year], nor with the setting of the London underground that it introduces. The deletion in this case strengthens the separating function of the refrain.

The most significant change in "Noche en claro" is the addition of a verb and the deletion of the period at the end. The last two verses of the 1962 text ("Ciudad Mujer Presencia / aquí se acaba el tiempo.") become three:

> Ciudad Mujer Presencia
> aquí se acaba el tiempo
> aquí comienza

[City Woman Presence
here time ends
here it begins]

By making the perception of time not only the terminal point
but also the point of departure, Paz uses the two extremes to
nullify each other in a timeless world. The timelessness is
graphically reinforced by the omission of the period with its
indication that a limit has been reached. Even more impor-
tant is the way in which the poem's new conclusion both
recalls the circularity of *Piedra de sol* and anticipates the
polarities of *Ladera este*. Thus the poet uses the revision in
two ways: to structure the poem into parts that further im-
pose upon the reader a requirement of meaning, and to define
the poem's objective as the joining of opposites and the aboli-
tion of time.

"Salamandra" is atypical in Paz's work for its choice of
subject from the animal world and for its approach, a series of
glosses on the symbolism and definition of this amphibian.
Since fifteen of the twenty stanzas begin with the animal's
name, giving the effect of an incantation, the poem is an
extended anaphora. In its unabashed risk of monotony, cata-
loging of qualities, exploration of definitions, and com-
parison of concepts, the technique seems to be traditional.
Yet taken together, these devices imply a diversification
rather than a repetition of meaning, in the same way that
Gertrude Stein's famous repetition of "rose" suggests that a
word conveys a different meaning every time that it is in-
voked.

There are two elements that are rather unconventional.
One is the exclusion of narrative from all sections of the
poem except the lengthy one incorporating the Aztec myth of
the *axolotl*. Equally significant—and perhaps derived from
the limitation of narrative—is the sparse use of action verbs,
so that the initial impression of the poem's composition as
one principally of nouns and adjectives is continued through-
out the reading. The effect of both of these devices is to assign
to the metaphors the burden of the poem's meaning.

Paz's imaginative treatment of the subject bridges a wide cultural, chronological, and geographical chasm by combining the traditional European symbolism of the salamander's association with fire and the Aztec myth of creation. The former originates in Pliny, who credits the salamander with the ability to quench fire with the coldness of its body; from this legend is derived its relationship to fire, both divine and demonic, and its connotation of chastity that keeps cool in the heat of passion.[2] This symbolism provides a common denominator for the entire poem except for the thirteenth stanza, verses 103-27, which is based on Aztec symbolism.

The latter is also concerned with the creation of fire (the Aztec god Xolotl was credited with having brought both man and fire from the underworld), but even more with the sacrifice that was needed to enable the sun to initiate its movement. Although Paz does not give his source for the myth, verses 103-15 correspond precisely with a passage from Sahagún's *Historia general de las cosas de Nueva España*.[3] The ordering of events is identical in the two texts, as are some of the repetitions, used effectively by Paz in verses 109-10.

The basic characteristic of the Aztec myth is the dual nature of the salamander, "el dos-seres" [the twin being]. Xolotl is at the same time a coward and a hero, whose death makes it possible for the sun to move. He is also both a dog and a man, a giver of life and the god of monstrosities. He is represented both by the butterfly (air) and the sea (water). As the twin of Quetzalcoatl, he is the dark side, the evening star, opposed to the god's presence in the morning star. He is the appropriate symbol, then, for the joining of opposites that recurs throughout Paz's poetry.

Paz's method of joining the two myths, by isolating the Aztec legend in the stanza of twenty-four verses that stands out from the shorter ones of twelve verses or less, gives the longer stanza a dominant position in the poem. He also calls attention to it by omitting the incantatory repetition of the animal's name that introduces all the other stanzas of the poem except a very brief definition (lines 101-2) and the final stanza (159-67). The two traditions, therefore, are merged in the poem and yet separated by the form.

Although all the poems of *Salamandra* begin with a cap-
italized first word, the heading here suggests a concept of the
subject that is maintained and developed throughout the
poem, the "objective" definition that might be found in an
encyclopedia or dictionary. Immediately contradicted—or,
rather, replaced—by the metaphor of verses 2 and 3, it is
extended by verse 4 ("calorífero de combustión lenta"),
which is a direct quotation from the dictionary of the Royal
Spanish Academy. At the same time, verse 4 represents a
continuation of the European legend of the salamander pre-
sented by the introductory metaphor. The same can be said
for verses 13-14. Two entire stanzas, beginning with verses 75
and 80, extend the factual and dispassionate observation of
the animal's characteristics, giving the impression that they
have been extracted from scientific works. They are con-
tinued by the parenthetical section of seven verses (94-100)
and the fragmentary stanza of two verses immediately fol-
lowing. After lengthy nonobjective developments, the scien-
tific description is resumed (or interrupts) in verses 145-48
and 159-61.

The latter section stands out for its simplicity of observa-
tion, particularly in its position as the introduction of the
final stanza and therefore the summary of the multiple and
supernatural character of the subject. The directness of these
verses ("La salamandra es un lagarto / su lengua termina en
un dardo" [The salamander is a lizard / his tongue ends in a
dart]) is stressed by the uniformity of verse length (nine
syllables not only for verses 159-61, but also for those imme-
diately preceding and following) and by the rhyme of *lagar-
to / dardo*. The impression of a child's point of view, if not of
doggerel, is reinforced by the repetition of "dardo" in 161.

A concealed use of the dictionary, which is combined with
the hermetic and surrealistic development of imagery, shapes
the beginning of the sixth stanza:

> Salamandra
> niña dinamitera
> en el pecho azul y negro del hierro

estallas como un sol
                    [lines 43-46]
[Salamander
        dynamite child
    in the black and blue breast of iron
    you explode like a sun]

This metaphor is related to an obscure definition of the
salamander in *Webster's Third New International Diction-
ary*: "an iron used red hot for igniting certain substances (as
gunpowder)." Since this definition is not listed by Spanish
dictionaries—or in fact by other English dictionaries—the
poet cannot have counted on the reader's knowledge of the
allusion. The reader must associate it, therefore, with the
legendary creature of fire rather than with the objective and
factual treatment of the subject.

Opposed to what we may call the scientific voice in the
poem is the larger and more complex concept of the sala-
mander as the essence of fire. In most of the stanzas that are
not dominated by literal description, the relationship of the
salamander with fire (or with the associated images of stars
and explosives) is explored.

The structure of the poem rests on the variety and unifor-
mity of the salamander's characteristics, developed in stan-
zas that are essentially nineteen separate poems on the
subject. Although the fleeting images of stanzas, 1, 2, and 4
make unity difficult, there is a compensatory clarity in
stanza 3, in which the salamander is a decorative note against
the stark backdrop of the modern city, and stanza 5, whose
common denominator is the salamander as a spark buried
within mineral depths. Unity is also apparent within stanza
6, whose explosive moment is characterized by the grouping
of three of the poem's rare action verbs. The seventh stanza
uses comparisons that are ethereal ("condensación," "subli-
mación," and "evaporación") in a development that seems
inconsistent with preceding or subsequent material. The
reader must provide unity for the poem if he finds it neces-
sary.

In "Salamandra," as in "Noche en claro," revisions of the text (1962) underline the process of depuration. In "Salamandra," too, Paz has divided a long poem into stanzas, enabling him to dispense with some of the parentheses (*Poemas*, 379, verse 103; 380, verse 127; 381, verses 145 and 148). The omission of three sets of parentheses in the first two stanzas (with the exception of verses 2 and 3) of the later version, however, responds to a different intention. All of them, following the pattern of the initial set that is retained, contain development of the salamander's resistance to fire, which contrasts with the nonparenthetical image of the salamander as an extension of fire. The revision thus joins the opposites that are clearly separated at the initiation of the poem and that continue to be separate in the earlier version.

A similar effect is achieved through the deletion of parentheses and the rearrangement of verses in the third stanza (*Poemas*, 377, verses 26-31). Here the verticality of verses initiated in the center of the line suggests two voices or at least two interlocking *haiku*. There is also a tension in the contrast (and balance) of the juxtaposition (and separation) of "amarilla" and "roja" in the same image. In both the first and third stanzas the elimination of parentheses implies that the simplification of the subject involves seeing mutually exclusive qualities as complementary.

The poet's task is concentrated on shaping the separate images evoked in the stanzas, of which only some provide coherence. The poem is built on the comparisons between the European and Aztec symbols, on the scientific and magical concepts of the subject, and on the tension between unified and fragmented imagery. The final effect is that of a large collection of metaphors evoked by the salamander which are effective to the degree that they are accepted. One has the impression that Paz consciously creates a loose construction which the reader can select from or disassemble or reassemble at will. Rather than reducing his theme to an essence, Paz has divided it in this poem into several, obliging the reader to share in the definition of meaning, which may not be final.

In its theme, structure, and form (particularly the combination of punctuated and unpunctuated verses), "Solo a dos voces" appropriately summarizes the volume that it closes. Its epigraph, taken from Corominas, *Diccionario crítico-etimológico de la lengua castellana*, suggests that the subject is the multiple meanings of language.

The first stanza anticipates in its polarities of "Sí" and "No" the principal technique of *Ladera este*. Its first ambiguity which is apparent only in recitation, is the contradiction between "Si" and "Sí." Equally important is the place of "Sí" (I,5) so that it applies equally to the preceding and following verses. The typographical arrangement of verses 9-10 suggests a meaning distinct from the same words used in verse 5, as, again, the ambiguous placement of "no" (I,8) is related to the two verses that surround it. What might have been the "final" question of verse 14 defining the principal subjects of the poem is overshadowed by verse 15, which stresses one of Paz's constant themes, the nature of language.

The double structure of the poem, which like "Himno entre ruinas" alternates two voices in contrasting types, boldface and italic, is reinforced by the difference in tone and logic of the first two stanzas. Where the first is contradictory, ambiguous, and intensely personal, the second, whose subject is the description of external reality, is reasoned, clear, and objective. Although very succinct in its first statement of only four verses, the second stanza portrays the poet's realistic consciousness of himself as he begins the task of formulating his experience. Most important, "yo escribo" (II,4) indicates that this voice is that of the poet aware of his mission.

The third stanza, now assisted by punctuation, continues the tone of the first and the development of the three subjects announced earlier, "Mundo Solsticio Invierno." In the contrast between the world and the sun, the sun is seen as a white-hot stationary point in space, opposite in character to the moveable world, personified in "dormida" and yet inanimate in the metaphor of verse 9. This contrast is developed in the final section of the stanza (II,10-14), with its repetitions and its word play of "pena" and "peña."

The fourth stanza continues the second's objective description of the rain falling in the patio. Now, however, with "Cae también en mi cuarto" [It falls in my room too], it affects the mood of the poet. The simile of II,5 establishes a link with the other voice of the preceding stanza. The dialogue between the two is anticipated by the poet's impression of the division of his personality, which the first voice reiterates in the final stanza of the poem (XIII,8).

The fifth stanza is characterized by the free associations and word play that were presented in the first, intensified by the alliteration of the second verse. The remainder of this stanza is a procession that is at the same time pagan and Christian, honoring Ceres and Nuestra Señora del Prado. The procession, the offerings of bread and candles, and the imagery of verses 10 and 21 are parallel. The alliterations of 14-17 and 18-19 unify and dramatize the ceremony. The final verse demonstrates in its simplicity and directness the joy of being a witness to life.

The first verse of the sixth stanza, a version of V,2, is clear in its comparison with poetry but obscure in its presentation of the subject. Why Ceres' body is "tres veces arado" [thrice plowed], whether she is also "la diosa negra" [the black goddess], and the symbolism of "caballo de agua" [horse of water] and "caballo de yerba" [horse of grass] are mysteries of a stanza that remains hermetic. Yet in its hermeticism, which is more characteristic of the first voice than the second, there is an element of structure, for it immediately follows the clarity of the other voice in the preceding stanza.

The seventh stanza returns to the subject of the procession celebrating the winter solstice. The first eight verses depict it in completely realistic terms. The image of the girls as "cántaros penantes" [suffering vessels], however, introduces a series of verses that are clearly understood separately but whose total meaning is elusive. The significance of the final three verses depends on the identity of "el hijo de la piedra incandescente" [the son of the incandescent stone].

Alternating obscurity with clarity, the poet in the eighth stanza struggles to write not a poem, but this one, as indicated by the series "palabras, muchachas, semillas, / sonido de guijarros" [words, girls, seeds / sound of pebbles]. Both the procession and the original presentation of the rain in the patio are recalled by verses 7-9.

The ninth stanza is an amplification of the first voice's initiation of the preceding stanza, "A solas con el diccionario" [alone with the dictionary]. Here the poet works in inverse alphabetical order, grouping words whose meanings present no pattern. His intention is to trace the point of origin, the source of the river of words, and to find the particle of energy that will be the essence of poetry.

The tenth stanza, the fifth of the voice that represents the consciousness of writing, portrays the void from which the poet must create meaning. He fights against the established directions, even the movement of the sundial. The indicator that might be considered reliable, the movement of the shadow cast by the sun, is false. The sun itself is a shadow, as unreliable as the one it casts.

If we consider the final verses of all the sections in italics, we can follow the trajectory of the poet struggling with expression: "yo escribo" [I write], "separado" [separated], "dibujar en la página / un caballo de yerba" [drawing on the page / a horse of grass], "Humedad y cemento" [Dampness and cement], "sol ido, / desvanecido, sol de sombra" [sun gone, / vanished, sun of shadow], and "la memoria es raíz en la tiniebla" [memory is a root in darkness.]

The theme of stanza 11 announces both the objective of this poem and its limits. In his explicit rejection of circular movement, the poet clarifies his desire to approach his subject, poetry, in another way. The use of "mundo mondo," more than word play, is a way of arriving at the essence of meaning. The different elements of the metaphor he is in the process of constructing ("mundo mondo, pulido como hueso, / decir es mondadura, / poda del árbol de los muertos" [unadorned world, polished like a bone, / saying is pruning, / pruning from the tree of the dead]) are both in denotation and connotation the process of reducing to essentials. The poet hopes that the reader's perception will go beyond the words of the poem: "Decir es . . . el no saber qué digo / entre la ausencia y la presencia / de este mundo" [Saying is . . . not knowing what I say / between the absence and the presence / of this world]. If the eleventh stanza is seen as the climax of the voice expressed in boldface type, the thirteenth and final stanza of the poem is an epilogue that develops further the emotion with which the poet has confronted the limits of his expression.

In the same way, the twelfth stanza, the final one of the voice expressed in italics, reaches the limit of the awareness of writing: "La letra no reposa en la página:" [The letter does not rest on the page:]. In this stanza the process is not so much a reduction as a disappearance, in which the letters are lifted by memory, "monumento de viento" [a monument of wind]. If the reader asks, as the poet does, who remembers memory, the answer is that identity dissolves, leaving only the brightness that is a root in the darkness. Memory, then, paradoxically, becomes disembodied, like poetry, and like this poem.

"Solo a dos voces" is typical of the approach to structure throughout *Salamandra*. By stating the limits of his own experience, frequently in the development of the poem rather than in its conclusion, Paz raises a fundamental question of meaning that cannot be left unanswered. The reader's response, outside the text of the poem, is the objective of the continued restatement and simplification of the subject.

4 *Blanco*
Multiple Meanings

¿La forma encierra un significado
o es únicamente un mecanismo de
significación que el lector pone
en movimiento?

[Does form contain a meaning or is
it only a mechanism for meaning
that the reader activates?]
        —Paz, *Poesía en movimiento*

More than most contemporary poems, irrespective of nationality, *Blanco* is difficult, complex, and ambiguous. Within the general challenge of Paz's production to date, this poem is the most inaccessible and the most demanding. If it is the clearest demonstration of Paz's theory that new poetry requires a new sensitivity from the reader and his active participation in the poetic process, *Blanco* may also offer the greatest rewards. Paradoxically for the critics, it may also be Paz's most deliberate attempt to illustrate his theory that the poetry of our age can be understood but not explained.

Perhaps the most important departure in this poem is its concentration on itself. A great many of Paz's poems, to be sure, are concerned with language and the writing of the poem. Here, however, as Gimferrer has pointed out more clearly than other critics, citing Breton's rejection of external themes, the poem takes its own composition as its major subject:

Pero, en el caso de Blanco, no sólo cuanto ocurre, ocurre en el poema, sino que únicamente alude a la realidad del poema, y lo que es más, los elementos de la realidad exterior al poema que aparecen en él (alusiones, por

ejemplo, al clima o a la orografía de México o la India) no
se encaminan a situarlo en el espacio o en el tiempo
externos a la escritura, sino que, por el contrario, tienen
por misión reforzar los datos textuales como tales, de
suerte que su función es exactamente inversa a la que
suelen desempeñar la metáfora, la metonimia y aun el
correlato objetivo.[1]

[But in the case of *Blanco* not only does everything that
takes place occur in the poem, but also only alludes to
the reality of the poem, and even more, the elements of
reality external to the poem that appear in it (allusions,
for example, to the climate or to the orography of Mex-
ico or India) are not directed to situate it in space or time
external to the text, but to the contrary, their objective
is to reinforce the textual information as such, so that
their function is exactly the opposite of the one usually
served by metaphor, metonymy, or even the objective
correlative.]

Because reality exists only in the text, Gimferrer equates
eroticism with writing, and vice versa. The feminine pres-
ence in the poem, therefore, is the word.[2]

Xirau stresses the multiple reading of the poem, for which
he finds antecedents in Mallarmé, Apollinaire, Pound, and
Cage, and, from older traditions, in Dante, Góngora, and
Provençal poets. In the presence of several readings, the read-
er is free to choose: *"Blanco* no se impone: se ofrece" [*Blanco*
does not impose itself: it offers itself]. The subject of the
poem is language. Xirau, like Paz, sees the function of modern
poetry as the creation of a significance for life and man
through the abolition of other realities: "Más que diálogo con
el mundo, *Blanco* quiere fundar el mundo del diálogo" [More
than a dialogue with the world, *Blanco* intends to establish
the world of dialogue].[3]

Franco emphasizes the nontranscendental nature of the
poem, whose meaning rests on the relationships of the vari-
ous elements. For her, *Blanco* is a mandala that avoids a final

meaning. The text continues to refer to its surface and to signs (and spaces) that disintegrate as soon as they are read: "Es un poema que no permite la trascendencia, que nos centra en el presente" [It is a poem that does not permit transcendence, that centers us in the present].[4]

Sucre essentially agrees with Franco's interpretation, developing the poem's portrayal of a reality in flux. For him, the mission of the poem is not to translate an external world, but to depict the incessant movement in which that world has disappeared. Writing is establishing signs that seek a meaning, so that they extend the blankness of the poem's title. The reader must adapt the poem to, and by, his personal experience. Understanding the poem, then, is not discovering a meaning, but making one possible.[5]

The effects on the reader of the poem's fluidity are developed eloquently by Enrique Pezzoni in " 'Blanco': La respuesta al deseo." The various combinations of texts reveal a metatext, an ultimate reading programmed by the poet. The reader, accordingly, does not have unlimited power of creation. The text, in flux, both evades and offers itself to the reader, opening different meanings to those who discover relationships.[6]

The most convincing evidence of what Gimferrer calls "lectura polivalente" [multiple reading] is that the foregoing critical opinions are mutually complementary rather than exclusive. They thereby reflect the intention and structure of the poem. Paz's introductory explanation of the different ways in which the poem may be read represents an invitation to a multiple reading. The definitions of the title itself can be grouped in terms of opposites, with "white" (a blank page) at one extreme, faced by its opposite, "target" (aim, objective, or object of desire). In this opposition the title is a paradox. The implication from Paz's suggested variant readings (total poem; central column as one poem; left- and right-hand columns read horizontally as four separate poems; each of the above sections read separately, making fourteen poems) is also one of opposition and antithesis. Although the introductory explanation runs counter to the objective of unrestrained response by the reader, it is indispensable.

Paz's suggested readings have a tone of symmetrical and mathematical logic that is derived from the poem's typographical arrangement in double columns, a central column, and, depending on the edition, separation of verses either by color or by a change of type.[7] The poet supplies further guidance by defining the character of the subpoems: the central column's theme is the passage of the word from sentence before speech to silence after it; the left-hand column is a love poem, divided into movements corresponding to the four traditional elements; and the right-hand column is a counterpoint to the left, composed of variations on sensation, perception, imagination, and understanding.

The poet's introduction, which in his extensive production has only the epilogue note to the first edition of *Piedra de sol* as an antecedent, is designed to stimulate the reader's imagination while providing a critical framework for the reading. For example, a completely mathematical combination of groupings would include a reading of all four double sections as a single poem, a possibility that Paz has not mentioned. This omission, which cannot be inadvertent, leads to a larger and more significant question: is the poet's list meant to be exclusive? If not, are there other subpoems that can be defined, such as the reading in reverse order of the various sequences, or the reversal of the right- and left-hand columns, or the combination of the central column with only one half of the double column sections?

The structure of *Blanco* makes an interesting comparison and contrast to *Piedra de sol.* The two poems are unconventional in their flexibility and innovative in their intention of abolishing linear form. In this respect both may be considered as the poetic parallel of Paz's essays developing the nonlinear concept of time, history, and the nature of man. But the methods of achieving this end differ in these two major poems. In *Piedra de sol* the structure is circular, so that while a fixed beginning and end are apparently abolished, the sequence of parts is retained. The development of one subtheme follows (or repeats, or is a variation on) another. The effect on the reader is to merge the parts into a circular unity, but in the reading of the poem itself, no part can be omitted.

In *Blanco,* on the other hand, all readings of the text as subpoems are predicated on the exclusion of certain sections. In this way the reader's full participation is invited not only in the ordering of reality, but also in the creation of the phenomena and the values which compose it. The subpoems of *Blanco* can be compared to blocks of the same size with different colors and textures. The patterns, although finite in number, are variable. We might apply here the architectural term "modular" to refer to the variety of design that can be achieved through the use of interchangeable parts. In contrast, the structure of *Piedra de sol,* consisting of circles, provides variety through differing points of view; no detail or section can be removed from within a given circle without damaging its structure and the unity of the poem.

In order to simplify reference to *Blanco,* the sections will be designated here by capital letters. The six single-column sections, therefore, are A, C, E, G, I, and J. The double-column sections are labeled in the same manner with the addition of the designations a for left and b for right columns. The omission of a or b indicates that the line should be read as one verse extending across both columns.

Like *Piedra de sol, Blanco* is a major poem developed between two polarities. In *Piedra de sol,* these were represented by the epigraph and the poet's note as epilogue. Here the opposition is embodied in the two brief epigraphs. The significance for Paz of Tantric Buddhism is amply developed in several critical essays.[8] In general, one of its main attractions for the poet is its ability to resolve opposites and to reconcile, if not abolish, the series of dualities (good and evil, appearance and essence, ends and means, body and soul, etc.) that distort man's perception of the world. Within the first epigraph there is another opposition developed, that of the world bound versus the world released, which raises the question whether passion that is the instrument of both enslavement and liberation is the same, or whether there are different kinds of passion, or whether the passion is the same but operative under opposing circumstances.

In opposition to the assertion of the Tantra, which as-

sumes realities of appearance and essence, is the second
epigraph's denial of reality ("Avec ce seul objet dont le Néant
s'honore" [With that single purpose with which Nothingness
is honored].[9] The implication is that of a highly organized
structure whose principles are negative and whose center is
nothing. Mallarmé's use of the capital of "Néant" is reveal-
ing. In his stimulating essay "Los signos en rotación," a
sequel to the esthetic credo of *El arco y la lira*, Paz defines the
significance of Mallarmé's denial, particularly in "Un Coup
de dés," for the general history of modern poetry. He views
Mallarmé's poem both as a condemnation of "idealist"
poetry—a rejection of any poetic effort to duplicate the
world—and a reaffirmation of poetry. Its novelty consists in
being a self-critical poem containing its own negation and
using it as a point of departure: "La negación de la negación
anula el absurdo y disuelve el azar" [The negation of negation
annihilates absurdity and dissolves chance].[10] More for what
it does than for what it states, "Un Coup de dés" closes an
epoch in modern poetry and inaugurates another.

Paz's observations on the interpretation of Mallarmé's
poem are helpful for the comprehension of *Blanco*. Beginning
with the declaration that Mallarmé's poetic language
achieves at the same time its greatest condensation and dis-
persion, he notes its escape from the tyranny of linear form.
Whether reading is done from left to right or vertically,

> las frases tienden a configurarse en centros más o menos
> independientes a la manera de sistemas solares dentro
> de un universo; cada racimo de frases, sin perder su
> relación con el todo, se crea un dominio propio en esta o
> aquella parte de la página y esos distintos espacios se
> funden a veces en una sola superficie sobre la que brillan
> dos o tres palabras.[11]

> [the phrases tend to arrange themselves in more or less
> independent centers like solar systems within a uni-
> verse; each cluster of phrases, without losing its rela-
> tionship to the whole, asserts its own authority in this
> or that part of the page and those different spaces are

occasionally fused into a single surface on which two or
three words gleam.]

The introduction of the first section of *Blanco* is the clear-
est example of poetic language and structure in flux. The
isolated nouns and adjectives float around each other ty-
pographically and semantically, suggesting a free association
of particles that have not yet assumed a pattern, or rather that
form several patterns that are subject to change. The most
obvious feature of the first thirteen lines is the absence of a
verb, which would necessarily supply a governing syntactic
and semantic sense of direction. The idea of genesis is stated
appropriately in the first verse, "el comienzo" [the fountain;
literally, the beginning], and developed through the associa-
tion of "el cimiento" [the founding], "la simiente" [the seed],
"la palabra en la punta de la lengua" [word on the tip of the
tongue], and "grávida" [gravid] to the repetition of "la pal-
abra" in A,13, which stabilizes the definition of the subject of
that whole section.

The graphic form of the first thirteen verses, comprising
the introductory section, is the extension of Paz's observation
of "Un Coup de dés" as "sistemas solares" and "racimos de
frases." Nor can it be coincidence that Paz's characterization
of Mallarmé's method as one in which "brillan dos o tres
palabras" is particularly apt here, where the words that stand
out, literally, are "la palabra" in two verses. Another grouping
of words and phrases, however, is suggested by the double-
column sections of *Blanco*. In section A, designated by the
poet as a single column, the typographical arrangement con-
sists of three columns in the first thirteen verses and of two
columns for the remainder. A similar division of the single
columns—into two, with a brief reappearance of three in
section I—occurs throughout the poem.

The introductory thirteen verses are set off from the rest of
the section not only by the tripartite column arrangement
referred to, but also by the absence of capital letters, which is
typical of the double-column sections. With the exception
noted here, all of the single-column sections follow the con-

ventional use of capital letters at the beginning of verses. The use of lower-case letters in the introduction also suggests the lack of a formal beginning—in contradiction to the denotation of the first four verses. The last two verses of the introduction, rejecting the powers associated with speech ("la palabra / sin nombre sin habla" [the word / nameless speechless] are a paradox. The poem, therefore, begins with an introduction that seems to deny itself.

The opening verses embody a search for language that is the theme of all the single-column sections. The search, dramatized by the echoing qualities of verses 2 and 4, broadens in both rhythm and meaning in verses 5 and 10. These serve as a framework for a complex relationship developed among the single words of verses 6 through 9. The subject, clearly, is the unenunciated word of verse 5. Yet "inaudible" denies "inaudita" as "nula" denies "grávida." Exactly between these two oppositions, between vertical and horizontal readings, is the center word "impar." In a direct vertical line below it, also impervious to, or neutralized by, opposing forces is "sin edad." After the broad, full horizontal line of 10, the epithet to verse 6, the same play of opposites takes place again. "Promiscua" balances "inocente," emphasizing the neutrality of "la palabra" in the center. With the exception of verse 13, which contains two negative synonyms, the left column is composed of positive and fruitful connotations, while the right is made up of their negative or sterile counterparts. The emphasis on the center words is consequently strong, so that "impar" and "sin edad" become the central attributes of "la palabra." The strength of the center words is also conveyed by the unusual typographical arrangement, so that the conventional linear sequence is enhanced by the additional dimension of verticality. "Impar" belongs impartially not only to the preceding and the following verses, but equally to each of the four adjectives:

inaudita		inaudible
	impar	
grávida		nula

    [unheard   unhearable
                        indivisible
     gravid   void]

In the same manner, "sin edad" belongs to "grávida" and
"nula" and is directly connected vertically to both "impar"
and verse 10. "La palabra" is the center of the new small
constellation of verses 11-13. The effect of reading the four
modifying expressions, isolated by rhythm and typography, is
to put "la palabra" in the center as the modifiers revolve.

Verses 14 through 18 form a separate unity within the
section. Because they consist of two short, simple, and con-
ventionally grammatical sentences, they are a transition be-
tween the verbal fragmentation of the introduction and the
three lengthy, rambling sentences that form the second half
of the first central column section. Their function as a transi-
tion is borne out by the typographical pattern, which leaves
these in one column, but returns to a suggestion of double
columns from 21 to the end of the section. Along with fully
developed syntax comes the personification of the first sen-
tence and the metaphor of the second. Both are attempts to
make language concrete, just as the word wandering through
the uninhabited halls of language seeks an exit, and just as
the rhythmic recurrence of light holds the promise of a con-
stant illumination. The synesthesia, alliteration, and ono-
matopoeia of "Late una lámpara" [A lamp throbbing]
emphasize the brevity of this verse in marked contrast to the
sinuous sentences that follow it.

The rest of this section is the construction of a large
metaphor: language creates its own reality as convincing and
observable as that of the sunflower. "Asciende" [It ascends]
recalls the search for exit of the first transitional sentence, as
"claridad" [clarity] does the light of the second. The words
and phrases whose arrangement suggests a right column can
be read separately as the essence of verses 19 through 43, a
shorthand transcript of the experience. Three phrases on the
left, near the conclusion, cast doubt on the accuracy of per-
ception: "ficticia" [fictitious], "ni vista ni pensada" [neither

seen nor thought], and "aparece" [it appears] suggest that the centrally placed "flor" [flower] and "amarillo" [yellow] are either unreal or super-real.

Held in a fictitious hand, the sunflower is a symbol for language, so that it must be heard in line 39 rather than perceived in the usual terms. The gulf between sign and meaning, another of the great dualities that the poet seeks to resolve, is abolished in the final five verses: the sunflower, first heard, is finally seen in its essential quality of yellow, not like, but actually made up of, consonants and vowels in flames. Using a metaphor, the poet has sought to abolish metaphor. Just as this section's introduction denied itself, so does its climactic symbol strive to destroy itself.

There are a number of details that subtly connect the single- and double-column sections of the poem. Each of the left columns, it will be recalled, is built around one of the traditional four elements. Section B, for example, represents fire. It is introduced by the last word of A, "incendiadas" [burning], anticipated in turn by "luz carbonizada" [carbonized light] of A,32. In the same way, but with more emphasis, water is introduced in C,2 ("sílabas húmedas" [humid syllables]) and repeated in C, 8, 11, 15-19, and particularly 38-41, just before it is presented as the leitmotif of section D. In like fashion, the earth of double column F is presented by single column E, and the air of double column H by G. Although variant readings may omit one or two of the themes on the elements, they cannot be excluded from the poem. Perhaps their most important function is their incorporation into the central-column theme of language and the unity they provide to it. It may not be excessive to suggest that their use in the central column makes language, if not the fifth element, at least a basic ingredient of life in general and the essence of man in particular.

The second single-column section, C, continues to develop the theme of language, now with a more personal connection with the poet. Language thus far has appeared only as something potential and imminent. Now the quotation from Livingston conveys a heroic tone and the bravery of hope against all odds. Here, as in other poems by Paz, water symbolizes the flowing of words that is poetry. Lines 9-13 recall the fire of section B to express the poet's sense of aridness. The Aztec hieroglyphic sign of ember and water, explained in one of Paz's notes to *Ladera este,* is not only a joining of opposites, but the introduction to the awareness of history. The drying up of inspiration is symbolized by the image of the clogged spring (lines 19-24). It is caused by the weight of history, and that reference also clarifies the meaning of the preceding lines (14-18): the poet is the victim not only of events but of his old enemy, time. His particular expiation is to write when he cannot write, to speak when it is impossible to speak. Although "pulir huesos" [to polish bones] may not seem to go beyond a trivial task, there is a penalty in making life out of the materials of death (21-22 and 35). The real nature of the poet's task takes on the dimension of mythological impossibility, again dramatized by the unexpected synesthetic perception, here of "Aguzar / silencios / Hasta la transparencia" [To sharpen / silences / To the point of transparency], mixing touch, sight, and hearing to end the section with a specific reference to the second element, and with a pause that denies itself, the colon.

The personal references of lines 4, 9, and 14 clarify the theme of the central columns and reinforce its significance with a new dimension. The poet is dealing not only with the abstraction of language in general—with esthetics and semantics—but also with his own powers of expression and with his ability to fulfill himself through his work. Language as "expiación" and "propiciación," therefore, suggests a mission as compelling as the religious rituals that both terms evoke.

In addition to looking forward to the next double-column section, F, through the introduction of the third element, earth (1-3, 21, 26-30), section E also looks backward to the two elements already developed fully in the previous double-column sections, fire and water. Fire is combined with earth in the first three verses:

Paramera abrasada
Del amarillo al encarnado
La tierra es un lenguaje calcinado.

[Charred moorland
From yellow to flesh colour
Earth is a burnt-out language.]

The same element reappears as the fury of the sun in lines
10-11. The heat of the landscape is dominant until the end of
the section (30-36), when rain brings a renewal both to the
landscape and the poet. Here again, the element being intro-
duced, earth, is combined with a previously developed one:

Te abres, tierra,
Tienes la boca llena de agua,
Tu cuerpo chorrea cielo,
[lines 30-32]

[You are opening
Earth your mouth full of water
Your body dripping with sky]

By means of this cumulative reference to the elements, the
central-column sections are given additional unity and at the
same time are connected with the double-column sections
from which they are at first glance so independent.

The third single-column section makes a further develop-
ment of the theme of language. In the first, language was felt
as a potentiality, a phenomenon in genesis. In the second, it
was felt as an anguish of the poet; filling its absence was his
task and the definition of his existence. Here it is still unre-
alized as a presence but referred to concretely in its identi-
fication with earth. Throughout the development (1-24) the
poet's attention turns to the arid landscape, whose connec-
tion with language is established in the third verse. The
storm that develops is as much that of the poet's frustration
in his struggle with language as it is a description of his

surroundings. The relief of rain, more than pictorial, is one of fulfillment for the poet, who uses metaphors of growth and fertility to signify full communication. In the brief but dramatic conclusion ("Verdea la palabra" [The word grows green]), language has arrived as a presence. With the color green and the repetition of "palabra," section G begins where E concluded. In this climax of the six single-column sections, there is a simultaneous fulfillment, both of language in general and of the poet's search for expression. Everything here expresses order, meaning, harmony and transcendence. Condensed here are Paz's theories on what poetry should be and do. In line 10, he alludes to the comprehension beyond thought; in 20, still using the contrast between "veo" and "pienso," he reverses the terms to suggest a comprehension beyond comprehension, one clearly that is felt rather than reasoned. One is reminded of Archibald MacLeish's conclusion to his "Ars poetica," that a poem "should not mean but be."

If, as Paz has defined it, the principal objective of poetry is to discover an ultimate reality behind the appearances of the world, if the main function of poetic language is not to communicate but create, section G realizes the poet's goals:

> La imaginación poética no es invención sino descubrimiento de la presencia. Descubrir la imagen del mundo en lo que emerge como fragmento y dispersión, percibir en lo uno lo otro, será devolverle al lenguaje su virtud metafórica: darle presencia a los otros. La poesía: busquedad de los otros, descubrimiento de la *otredad*.[12]

> [Poetic imagination is not the invention but the discovery of presence. To discover the image of the world in what emerges as fragment and dispersion, to perceive the one in the other, will be to restore to language its metaphoric capability: to give presence to others. Poetry: searching for others, discovery of *otherness*.]

All of section G, particularly the two key words "Traslumbramiento" [Splendour] and "Aerofanía" [Diaphaneity], expresses transcendence. In lines 1-9 language surpasses itself in glories of color, light, and movement. "Traslumbramiento" refers as much to the lines preceding it as to the lines beyond the colon. The formulation of ultimate reality is based on a rejection of reality, on a comprehension beyond normal terms of perception:

> no pienso, veo
> —no lo que veo,
> Los reflejos, los pensamientos veo.
> [lines 10-12]
>
> [I do not think, I see
> —Not what I see
> I see reflections, thoughts.]

Only the circuitous use of words can reach their essence. Yet having reached the goal, the poet has difficulty conveying his feelings (poetry does not convey or communicate), so that lines 20-21 are another double rejection of the transcendence he has just defined. Now it is expressed in terms of absences, silences, and nonappearances, including one which recalls the poem's title:

> —no lo que pienso,
> la cara en blanco del olvido,
> el resplandor de lo vacío.
> Pierdo mi sombra,
> avanzo
> entre los bosques impalpables,
> las esculturas rápidas del viento,
> los sinfines,
> desfiladeros afilados,
> avanzo,
> mis pasos
> se disuelven
> en un espacio que se desvanece
> en pensamientos que no pienso.
> [G,21-34]

                    —not what I think
            blank face of forgetfulness,
            the radiance of the void.
        I lose my shadow,
                    I advance
            among impalpable woods,
            rapid sculptures of the wind,
            along the endless,
                        sharp-edged paths,
            I move,
                    my steps
                        dissolve
            in a space that vanishes
            in thoughts I do not think.]

The aims that Paz proposes for poetry in general are particularly applicable to this moment of fulfillment in *Blanco:*

> Toda creación poética es histórica; todo poema es apetito por negar la sucesión y fundar un reino perdurable. Si el hombre es trascendencia, ir mas allá de sí, el poema es el signo más puro de ese continuo trascenderse, de ese permanente imaginarse.[13]

> [Every poetic creation is historical; every poem is a hunger to deny succession and found a permanent kingdom. If man is transcendence, going beyond himself, the poem is the purest sign of that continual transcending, of that permanent imagining.]

With section I the poet returns to the triple arrangement of the central column that characterizes section A. Appropriately, the first phrase, "En el centro," is placed in that position to introduce the tripartite symbolism of line 2. Here there is a deliberate ambiguity dependent on whether the line is read as an accumulation of possessives or as a series in apposition. In either case, the double column of line 3 symbolizes an illumination of meaning. "Resplandor," which forms one of the central paradoxes of the preceding section, establishes continuity between G and I. Also in the center, the "No" of line 4 is so large a denial as to reverse not only the first three lines of this section, but the paradise gained of section G. The "remolino" in which the word gloriosly appeared in that section is reversed here to become "el remolino de las desapariciones." Appearances are a whirlwind that is affirmed, the tree of names is denied, as "Sí" and "No" alternate. The "No" of line 9 has two additional interpretations, with "Árbol" as subject or with "No" itself as subject, in which it gains a positive value. In the same way, "Sí" of 11 may be read by itself or as the subject of line 12. Both "Sí" and "No" prepare the reader for the ambiguities of unpunctuated lines 13-14 ("Aire son nada / Son") which in turn introduce the fragments of observation that constitute the central part of the section (15-40).

The final central column (section J) contains a philosophical riddle that explains the return of what seems to be chaotic enumeration and justifies the abandonment of the harmonious vision of section G:

Si el mundo es real
               La palabra es irreal
Si es real la palabra
               El mundo
Es la grieta el resplandor el remolino
No
         Las desapariciones y las apariciones
                       Sí
          [lines 44-51]

[If the world is real
               The word is unreal
If the word is real
               The world
Is the crevice the dazzle the whirlwind
No
         The disappearances and the appearances
                       Yes]

The implication here is that the world and language cannot coexist as realities.

Lines 47-55 recapitulate symbols of this section's introduction, denying each other until everything is canceled out. Their function is to develop an eloquent silence:

> El habla
>> Irreal
> Da realidad al silencio
>> Callar
> Es un tejido de lenguaje
>> Silencio
>> [lines 56-61]
>
> [Speech
>> Unreal
> It lends reality to silence
>> Stillness
> Is a fabric of language
>> Silence]

Yet if silence, both of language and of the poet's search for expression, is the final poem, it is founded on a paradox, for there can be no silence if there is no speech (line 69). This is the final—both positional and logical—explanation of the poem, which is different from its conclusion.

The entire last part of this section, beginning with the assertion of opposites crystalized in "Sí" and "No," can be summarized as a return to silence. Yet, as both the poet and the poem assert, there are different kinds of silence, and the one after speech, at the end of the poem, differs radically from the one before speech. The distinction is provided by the reader, and the result is a new form of poetic expression:

> Entre la página y la escritura se establece una relación, nueva en Occidente y tradicional en las poesías del Extremo Oriente y en la arábiga, que consiste en su mutua interpretación. El espacio se vuelve escritura: los blancos que respresentan al silencio, y tal vez por eso

mismo, dicen algo que no dicen los signos. La escritura proyecta una totalidad pero se apoya en una carencia; no es música ni es silencio y se alimenta de ambos.[14]

[Between the page and the writing there is established a relationship, new in the West and traditional in Far Eastern and Arabic poetries, that consists in their mutual interpretation. Space becomes writing: the blanks that represent silence, and perhaps for that very reason, say something that the signs do not say. The writing projects a totality but rests on an absence; it is not music or silence and is nourished on both.]

The technique of section J, anticipated at the conclusion of I, is one of evaporation. Beginning with a circular syllogism, the relationship between body, world, and spirit, the poem is both interrupted and continued by the polarity of "No" and "Sí" (line 7). These, in turn, preside over the remainder of the section, although there is no need to restate them. Beginning with lines 34 (a repetition of the penultimate verse of H) and 35 (the last line of D) through 44-46 (the repetitions of the conclusion of B and F) to the final verse, section J attempts to express in a fragmentary way that both language and this poem say everything and say nothing. It is particularly significant that this development takes place between two lines that repeat the conclusion of H, of which the second becomes the final verse of the poem:

> La irrealidad de lo mirado
> Da realidad a la mirada

> [The unreality of the seen
> Makes real the seeing]

In this way, the subject of the final verse is not only the closest one, "Tu cuerpo" (line 48), but also all of the "irrealidad de lo mirado" announced in line 34.

The duality of the subject of the central-column sections, language and the love poem, results in separate conclusions.

Silence for language is achieved, paradoxically, in its fullest expression at the end of section I. Section J develops the theme as a gloss on the conclusion of the preceding section. "Tus pasos" (line 36) [your steps], "Estás desnuda / como una sílaba" (40-41) [You are naked / as a syllable], and the climactic "Tu cuerpo / Derramado en mi cuerpo" "(49-50) [Your body / flowing through my body] are the basis for an erotic vision that has been fulfilled. Yet, though they seem different, both conclusions represent the culmination of the poet's experience.

The theme of language is part of the continuing movement outward that we have been observing through the poet's work, which turns the reader's attention to ideas that can be reached only through readings outside the poem. In this case, the broader subjects of semantics and esthetics, derived from Paz's own wide knowledge in this area, necessarily lead the reader to philosophical considerations.

At the same time, the personal reaction to the poem, both the poet's and the reader's, is an inward movement, an emotional reaction that becomes progressively more difficult to generalize on. The more successful the poem is, the more deeply it is felt, the greater is the problem of conveying the meaning. The nature of this dilemma can be seen in Paz's commentary on typography:

> La página, que no es sino la representación del espacio real en donde se despliega la palabra, se convierte en una extensión animada, en perpetua comunicación con el ritmo del poema. Más que contiene a la escritura, se diría que ella misma tiende a ser escritura. Por su parte, la tipografía aspira a una suerte de orden musical, no en el sentido de música escrita sino de correspondencia visual con el movimiento del poema y las uniones y separaciones de la imagen. Al mismo tiempo, la página evoca la tela del cuadro o la hoja del album de dibujos; y la escritura se presenta como una figura que alude al ritmo del poema y que en cierto modo convoca al objeto que designa el texto.[15]

[The page, which is only the representation of the real
space in which the word unfolds, is converted into an
animated extension, in perpetual communication with
the rhythm of the poem. More than containing the text,
one would say that it itself tends to be the text. For its
part, typography aspires to be a kind of musical order,
not in the sense of written music but of a visual parallel
to the movement of the poem and the unions and sepa-
rations of the image. At the same time, the page evokes
the canvas or the page of the sketchbook; and the text is
presented as a figure that alludes to the rhythm of the
poem and that in a certain way convokes the object that
the text designates.]

There could be no clearer explanation than the above of
Paz's procedure in *Blanco,* yet the terms are necessarily
vague. The page as music, the page as painting, are inherently
projections of reader reactions that are infinitely varied.
Quite deliberately, Paz defines poetry here as a process that
draws the reader within—and, he hopes, beyond—his own
sensibilities and awareness.

A significant repetition in the introductions of the last two
sections (I, 1-13 and J, 1-12) draws attention to the relationship
among world, body, and spirit, three independent and yet
interdependent realities. Their correspondence to the divi-
sions in the poem is clear. The body is the left-hand column of
the double sections, and its immediate opposite, on the right,
is spirit, in the special definition Paz gives of "no-cuerpo."[16]
What is apparent from the circularity of the triple syllogism
on spirit, body, and world, exactly in the center of J (lines 27-
33), is that any one can be taken as the poem's center. Here,
briefly, Paz refers to the circularity of *Piedra de sol,* which he
does not specifically invoke, and of the mandala, which he
does.

Whether or not it is the center of reality, the center-column
section affords a separate vision from that of body and spirit.
The world by definition is neither physical nor spiri-
tual, although it might be a fusion of the two. In *Blanco,* as we

have seen, the world is language. In this definition, Paz has summed up both language's function as phenomenology and the power it gives to its instrument, the poet, as creator. For the individual, whether reader or poet (ideally, Paz feels, the distinction between them should be abolished), language is the means through which the world is perceived; for society, language is the means by which the world is created.

Like all the double-column sections, the first omits the use of capitals at the beginning of all lines except the concluding one, which, centrally placed, joins the preceding two columns and introduces the following center-column section. The suggestion here, as in section A, is that of a beginning in the middle of a development, which conveys a sense that something has preceded.

The element which the poet assigned to this section is projected in two levels of reality:

> en el muro la sombra del fuego
> en el fuego tu sombra y la mía
> [B,1-2a]
>
> [on the wall the shadow of the fire
> in the fire your shadow and mine]

The fire has a magical power over reality, both to conjure up and dispel, converting the figure of the girl into three symbols, grouped in B,5a without punctuation: "Pan Grial Ascua" [Bread Grail Ember]. Each in turn represents an essence of life. It may not be exaggerated to see in the three the trinity that figures so importantly in the poem: body, spirit, and world. "Muchacha" is made their equivalent and their summation, but is also seen independently through its placement in the isolated line following. At the same time, its position there makes it the subject of 7a and 8a. The end of the description (8a) leaves the reader undecided about which fire, and which girl, is more real.

The final line of this section, both for its capitalization and its position in the central column, is a reversion to the form of Section A. In the fire of both "pasión" and "brasa," it is a summation of the element to which this section is dedicated.

"Pasión," furthermore, recalls the first epigraph, drawn from the Tantra. Exactly why the ember is "compasiva," however, is not clear. Perhaps the term is used not in the usual sense to express pity, but in the connotation of its etymology, so that it signifies "con pasión," an accompaniment of passion. The ember, then, is a projection of the separate passions of man and woman ("tu sombra y la mía") and at the same time a symbol of an enveloping emotion in which everyone and everything participates.

In the second section of double columns (D), the passion has progressed from sight to bodily union. Here too the element, water, reveals a new dimension of reality. Just as the fire projected different levels in the shadows on it and the shadows it cast, so does the water show different kinds of reflections. The mirror and the "agua despierta" (8-9) are active, conscious participants in the poet's thoughts. The result of the poet's awareness is cast in terms that are recurrent in Paz's work:

> me miro en lo que miro
> como entrar por mis ojos
> en un ojo más límpido
> me mira lo que miro
> [lines 11-14]

> [I see myself in what I see
> like entering through my eyes
> into another more limpid eye
> what I see looks at me]

A major difference from other passages of such awareness, however, is the absence of limitation and frustration. Previously the image of reflecting awareness was a symbol of the barriers of perception and language that could not be crossed. Here the poet has gone beyond, "to the other shore," to a clearer vision of the world and of his place in it. As he has gone beyond the act of seeing to a purer vision, so has he transcended passion to reach a greater feeling, combined with symbols of water (lines 15-16).

The climactic line of this section, like that of Ba, suggests through capitalization and typographical position its relationship to the center-column sections. Also like its predecessor in Ba, this line is of greater length (eleven syllables, the same as B,9) than any other in the section. Clearly, also, it is a summation of the symbolism expressed by the element: transparency is all that remains, but nothing more is needed. Again, a goal has been reached, so that the separate character of Da, like that of Ba, is justified.

Section Fa, the third in the series devoted to the body, differs in several respects from the preceding left-hand sections. Although it still has a separate formal existence, indicated by italics, from its counterpart Fb, the space between columns present in B and D has been eliminated. Its presiding element, earth, is presented less explicitly, implied in 2a, 10a, and 12a, and stated only in 11a. This element, in fact, is suggested more by association with Fb. Furthermore, there is a syntactic indecision that does not characterize the other parts of the same series: uncertainty about the subject of the verbs in 1a and 2a (resolved in favor of "Ídolo"), followed by an omission of verbs for the remainder of the section, including the final verse.

What characterizes this section, even more than its sequel H, is the fusion of sensuality and philosophical abstraction. Passion is converted into an ideology. The explicitness of lines 7a-8a, for example, is transformed into "pirausta nudo de presencias" (9a) [fiery butterfly knot of presences]. In "mis manos de lluvia / sobre tus pechos verdes / mujer tendida" (F,13-15) [my hands of rain / on your green breasts / spread-out woman], sensuality, the subject of the center-column sections, is elevated to the level of phenomenology, indicated here once again by the center positioning and capitalization of the conclusion, "El mundo haz de tus imágenes" [The world a bundle of your images].

Much of the impact of this section's conclusion derives from the reversal of a traditional metaphor, in which the beloved sums up the meaningful qualities of life. Here the world is a reflection, not of the image, but of the multiple images of the beloved. Both the unity of the world and the diversity of its projections are conveyed by the final verse of this section. Even the most sensual vision of life becomes abstract and philosophical in Paz, which does not mean that it is any less personal. On the contrary, the culmination of the four sections on body in speculation on the meaning of life is a way of showing the unity, rather than the separation, of body and spirit.

In H, the double-column sections reach their lengthiest, fullest, and most climactic development. The final element, air, is suggested early in the section by the falling from body to shadow, extended through lines 2 and 3, in which the repetition of "sombra" ("de tu sombra a tu nombre") and the internal rhyme with "nombre" carry out the image of "cascada," as do the further repetitions of line 5. Other key words pertaining to air are borrowed from the right-hand column, printed without spatial separation in the first twenty lines: "las disipadas fábulas del viento" (7b) [the scattered fables of the wind]; "espacio dios descuartizado" (9b) [space carved out god]; "el firmamento es macho y hembra" (12b) [the firmament is male and female]; and "espacio es cuerpo signo pensamiento" (15b) [space is body sign thought].

The falling is also a symbol of passion at its climax, sweeping away the merged identity of the lovers:

> derramada en mi cuerpo
> tu te repartes como el lenguaje
> tu me repartes en tus partes
> ....
> entera en cada parte te repartes
> tu cuerpo son los cuerpos del instante
> visto tocado desvanecido
> [8-10a, 18-20a]

> [overflowing into my body
> parts of yourself you divide as speech
> me you divide in your gift of parts
> ....
> in each part of you you give yourself whole
> the bodies of the instant are your body
> seen touched vanished]

In the penultimate strophe of this section, the aftermath of passion is the listing and contrasting of the five sensory perceptions. Instead of utilizing them traditionally, the poet expresses transcendence through synesthesia. Ears see, eyes smell, smell caresses, the tongue hears, and touch tastes (21-25). As the senses are crossed, so are the two identities (26-27), merging in contrasts, contradictions, and resolution of opposites in the two concluding lines, whose importance is stressed by making them the anticipation of the final section of the entire poem.

In the first of the four counterpart sections to the body, the right-hand columns which Paz classified as sensation, perception, imagination, and understanding, the metaphor of sensation is explicit—"ánima entre las sensaciones" (B,3b)— and is emphasized by its solitary position without a corresponding line in B,3a. This verse summarizes the theme of the brief Bb section. Using the same element that is developed in Ba, fire, the poet depicts the soul as both besieged by threatening flames and yet liberated, just as in the first two verses the flame is surrounded by lions and the lioness is surrounded by flames. Opposing forces of sensual perception are thus combined in one sentence (the section has only one action verb form, "se abren") that is one experience.

When read horizontally in combination with Ba, the right-hand column not only amplifies it, but acquires a greater depth of its own. The subjects of the right column, of course, change. Instead of referring to "ánima," "llama," and "leona," lines B1-2b extend the two kinds of shadows of B1-2a. The dual nature of sensation, both besieging and liberating, of Bb illuminates a line of Ba ("el fuego te desata y te anuda" [the fire unties and ties you], which the poet emphasizes as the key line of the section on the body by placing it in the same isolation that he has given to B,3b. The three symbols of body, world, and spirit (B,4a) are now the apposition of "frutos de luces de bengala" [firework fruits]. The cause of the opening of the senses ("Muchacha") is specified; it is not the spontaneous action suggested when the right column is read by itself. In the same manner, there is now in 7a and 7b a connection between the sensual nude and the magnetic night.

The final line of the section (B,9) clearly is a summary of both columns. We have already commented on the unique capitalization and typographic position that relate it to the "neutrality" of the central columns. It unites the passion of body with the passion of sensation; it is both the object and the viewing of the object, utilizing the element that is the common denominator of both columns.

In Db, as in Bb, there is a lengthy enumeration that withholds the verb until the second half of the section. Here too, the element that forms the theme of the left column is also a vital part of the right column. What differentiates this section from the preceding, primarily, is not only the theme of perception but the extent of its development. In Bb there is only a beginning of the process leading to knowledge: the first "spiritual" section is, like the introduction of the poem, a depiction of genesis. In his first rudimentary awareness, the poet can only feel. If the process is generalized, man's knowledge has its origin in feelings.

In Db the second stage of awareness is defined. Through "el río de los cuerpos" [the river of bodies] in the first verse, the poet establishes a transition from the passion of the first section. As happens frequently in Paz's poetry, the full meaning of the enumeration that follows becomes clear only at its conclusion, when its function as subject or object of verbs is disclosed. When the right column here is read alone, the enumeration is seen as a puzzling series of abstractions with emphasis on a widening movement, particularly in the heavens: the river of bodies has become a river of suns. Only with the second stanza, in which the poet declares concretely that he is viewing his own creation (the reader remembers the comparison Paz makes in other poems between his writing and a river) does the enumeration of the first stanza gain perspective.

Even more important to the development of the right columns is the second verse of the second stanza, for it implies that reality is created by self-critical awareness: "la percepción es concepción" (D,12b), so that not only his work but even the poet himself, is created by seeing. Perception, then, is specifically the creative consciousness aware of its own action. The conclusion consists of two complementary verses that combine the truth of perception with water.

As the subjects and modifiers change position when the verses are read horizontally, both columns gain meaning. What was chaotic enumeration on first reading becomes a series of appositions that amplify the text on the body. Two verses in particular, dealing with "ti" and "mí" (D,3 and 6), acquire clarity when read horizontally. In the same way the second stanza achieves a depth of perspective that neither half possesses alone. Its first and last lines, which are mirror reflections in both cases of subject and object, suggest an infinite dimension that is often associated with Paz's use of the mirror.

The concluding line, like that of B, joins the two columns in an impersonal manner that bridges the gap between body and spirit. It is the essence of the element, water, to which the section is dedicated. As passion remained a symbolic ember previously, so here is the transparency of awareness the final symbol.

Section Fb, approximately the same length of Db, introduces a novelty in form: although the two halves are separated by different typefaces—and in the first edition by different colors—the space between them has disappeared, so that the natural inclination to read the two sections horizontally comes before the study of the separate halves. The absence of verbs noted in Fa after line 2 is remedied in part by the actions supplied in F,3-4b. From 5 on, however, the lack of verbs is prominent in both halves for the remainder of the section. If the right column in general represents spirit (or the term Paz would prefer, non-body), it is also the commentary of the poet on material reality, symbolized in this poem by the body. It is appropriate in this section, in which the spiritual half develops the subject of imagination, that the essential unity between the two halves should be indicated by the absence of the space division.

The right half of section F represents the same disconnection that was noted in the left half. But in the right it is more justifiable, for it is the depiction of the leaps of imagination itself, like the flight of the hawk, the goat poised to jump, the snapshot of one pulsation of time, all cited by the poet. Once again, he resorts to the conflict between opposites to express what one of the terms by itself could not: "real irreal quieto vibrante" (F,9b) [real unreal quiet vibrant].

The final line of the section has the same summarizing form and philosophical breadth that characterize the conclusions of the preceding sections. Together with the penultimate line, it bridges the separate functions of the two halves and reconciles them. As "mujer tendida" symbolizes all of the feelings connected with body, so does "hecha a la imagen del mundo" [made in the image of the world] describe the function of the imagination. "El mundo haz de tus imágenes," with its repetition of "imagen" of the penultimate verse, fuses body (world) with spirit in a comment on the nature of ultimate reality.

The final double-column section, both for its greater length (almost twice that of sections B and D) and its combination of separated and joined columns, is the climax of this group. The full development of its form is appropriate to the authority of its theme, understanding. Continuing the construction of reality by the imagination that was the theme of the preceding double-column section, the first lines here constitute a transition between the two:

> *no allá sino en mis ojos*
> *cielo y suelo se juntan*
> *intocable horizonte*
> *yo soy tu lejanía*
> [H,1-4b]
>
> *[not there but in my eyes*
> *sky and earth unite*
> *untouchable horizon*
> *I am your distance unfolding]*

The rest of the right column on understanding, paradoxically, is one of the most opaque passages in the poem. Clearly space and time are the subjects, and sexual metaphors (H,12-14b) recall the body theme of the left column. Read horizontally, the passage, like the preceding ones, acquires both a more comprehensible syntax and a more logical meaning. The effect of the supplementary reading on the right exceeds the modest classification of commentary that the poet assigned to it. In H,1, for example, the fall from body to shadow, which by itself requires a new spatial dimension, is extended by 1b, "no allá sino en mis ojos." In the second verse, in which the falling like a cascade is interrupted by the paradoxical modifier "inmóvil," a wider dimension is given to the action by including the joining of earth and heaven. As the falling continues in 3, imitating the form of the cascade, it is extended to an "intocable horizonte." The further leap of H,4a is projected into the poet's awareness of distance in H,4b. The method of extending each state of the fall accumulates through H,7. In general, in the remainder of this section the lines of the right column continue to extend the vision, the space, or the feeling of the left column. In this sense, they are projections of the left column, not a repetition of its basic meanings.

In the final two stanzas of the section, the poem reverts to the spatial division of the two columns that characterized the first two double-column sections. Although the poet may have been motivated in part by a desire for symmetry, there is perhaps a more compelling reason in the differentiation of function. Here the right column is not an extension of the left but a variation on it. Lines 20-25b, particularly, are five vivid metaphors for the synesthetic descriptions of 20-25a.

The concluding couplet is a series of interlocking paradoxes, the device preferred by Paz to express what is basically inexpressible. Verse 28 contains an opposition between unreality and the assumed reality of what is seen. This is compounded by making unreality the source of reality, which negates the unreality of the first line.

If the unity of the double-column sections is more apparent than each of the columns read separately, still another way of reading the poem comes to mind. As was noted previously, an obvious combination omitted by the poet in his introduction was the reading of the four double-column sections together. Yet there is nothing in these, as a unit, that goes counter to the intentions of the other readings of the poem or to the text as a whole. It seems safe to conclude that the poet did not intend to exclude the reading of the four as a separate unit and that, in fact, it is implied in his description of the four as independent units.

In one sense the final section of the poem is truly a conclusion:

> Pero el instante inmovilizado, el punto de fijeza desde el que se dispara *Blanco*, es este momento en una noche tranquila con unos pasos en el cuarto de al lado. Aquí se enlazan en un movimiento de unidad final, todos los temas del poema: la complimentariedad de los opuestos, las relaciones entre silencio y la palabra, entre página y mundo visible, entre realidad e irrealidad, entre percepción y experiencia fenomenológica, entre lenguaje y cuerpo y elementos.[17]

> [But the immobilized moment, the fixed point from which *Blanco* is fired, is this moment in a quiet night with footsteps in the neighboring room. Here all the subjects of the poem are bound in a movement of final unity: the complementarity of opposites, the relationships between silence and words, between page and visible world, between reality and unreality, between perception and phenomenological experience, between language and body and elements.]

The repetition in this section (with some alterations and in a different order) of the final verses of the double-column sections stresses their summarizing function.

Yet if we examine these repetitions and their context in the final section, what is emphasized is their impermanence and their ambivalence. "La transparencia es todo lo que queda" (line 35) [all that remains is transparency] not only makes its own statement of insubstantiality, but follows immediately

the polarities of "No   Sí / irrealidad de lo mirado." The
"pasión de brasa compasiva" (44) can last no longer than the
ember itself. "El mundo / haz de tus imágenes" could offer
permanence only if those images were clearly defined and
unchanging, but their appearance in the poem has been en-
tirely the opposite. What traditionally might be most objec-
tive in the concluding verse is, paradoxically, what is most
subjective; the body that "da realidad a la mirada" is at the
same time "visto" and "desvanecido." The restatement of
antitheses and paradoxes is not designed to confront the
reader with a sense of futility, but rather to challenge him to
supply an interpretation based on his own feelings rather
than those of the poet.

By not concluding the poem, Paz forcefully invites the
reader to continue the poet's task. In fact, the complexities of
the structure, particularly the multiple ways in which the
parts and readings can be assembled and disassembled, pre-
cisely contradict the first effect of the prefatory note. The
instructions create the impression that the poem is a finished
work, carefully crafted so that its modular elements may be
combined in certain patterns. Accustomed to traditional ap-
proaches, the reader can only assume at first that he faces a
closed work to which he can respond in different ways. Only
as he rereads the text does he learn that by seeing the relation-
ships between the parts, he does not recreate the poem so
much as he creates it. He is, accordingly, invited to write the
conclusion that is lacking in the text.

Although Paz's works examined so far have three distinct
structural patterns, they share a common theme in the ques-
tions they ask (rather than answer) about the human condi-
tion. In its conclusion-beginning, *Piedra de sol* forces man to
adopt a perspective outside himself to view his most intimate
nature. *Salamandra* presents—repeatedly and intensively—
changing perceptions of the world, with the irresistible im-
plication that they have no meaning except what man confers
on them. *Blanco* provides an elaborate structure which has
many variations. Once the reader has become aware of its
flexibility and complexity, he has gone beyond communica-
tion with the poet to stand on the threshold of his own poem.

5 *Ladera este*
Polarities

(The situation must be Yes-and-No,
                             not either-or)
                    —Paz, "Lectura de John Cage"

Paz's critics agree that *Ladera este* [*Eastern Slope*] should be viewed first in the biographical context suggested by the title, particularly the poet's years in diplomatic service in India (1962-68), where most of its poems were written. A number of studies show Paz's indebtedness to the East, seen not only in the subjects of the poems but also in themes shaped by Tantric philosophy. Tantrism certainly intensifies the use of eroticism that is dominant in this work. Xirau observes also the introduction of irony and the serious purpose behind it: "Y toda su poesía, religiosamente, adquiere el sentido de una plegaria (teísta o no), dirigida al mundo, a los signos del mundo, a las palabras y al fundamento indecible—musical, poético—de las palabras"[1] [And all his poetry, religiously, acquires the sense of a prayer (theist or not) addressed to the world, to the signs of the world, to words and the inexpressible foundation—musical, poetic—of words].

Ladera este represents not so much a change of direction for Paz as a new method. In this book, as in *Blanco*, he depicts the complexity of reality, which the reader achieves through participation in the creation of the poem. The theme of the poem extends beyond the text to the reader's reactions after completing the reading. In *Blanco* the process is based on the complexities of the text, revealed in part by the poet's instructions on the different ways in which the poem may be read. Although the reader is left free to follow wherever the poetic road may lead him, many lanes are clearly marked. The first part of the process, although complicated, is finite and programmed.

In *Ladera este*, the programming is more limited, so that the reader must use his own resources sooner. The devices of *Blanco* (for example, absence of punctuation, columnar structure, and ambiguous placement of words and verses) are employed extensively in this volume to stimulate the reader's reactions. Unlike the preface to *Blanco*, the notes to *Ladera este*, although helpful, are not indispensable. The effect is to challenge the reader's self-reliance by eliminating guidelines. For that reason, *Ladera este* makes excessive demands on the uninitiated. The analysis of four major poems may illustrate the unique character of this volume.

The success of "Vrindaban" rests on the numerous ways in which its subject, structure, tone, metaphors and theme contribute to different but simultaneous readings of the poem. Unlike many modern poets who cultivate ambiguity so that a poem can be interpreted in one way or another, Paz writes so that his poems mean one thing *and* another, or, better, several things. "Vrindaban" exemplifies the unity of *Ladera este*, whose poems are joined by an underlying multiplicity that becomes more significant than the uniformity of their subjects, drawn mainly from Indian geography. This multiplicity is in itself a connection with the essence of Indian culture that the book reflects.

The subject of the poem lays the ground for several interpretations. The poet writes at night, recalling his return home from a visit to an Indian temple, where he encountered a holy man, a *sadú*. Attempting to record the meaning of his experience, he is aware of his own finiteness, and particularly of the act—and the limitations—of writing. He seems to leave unresolved the basic questions that he formulates about the meaning of the *sadú*'s life and of his own.

The structure suggests a spiral in its recurrence to the awareness of writing with which the poem begins. The absence of punctuation stresses the importance of the introductory verb, which is immediately repeated ("Escribo me detengo / Escribo" [I write I stop / I write]). The aside that follows, whose contradictory functions are indicated by the separating parentheses and a continuation of the awareness of writing, introduces the main subject, the poet's recall of the night's previous events, which is interrupted again by a parenthetical phrase (line 21-25) about writing. A final parenthetical declaration, "aquí intervienen los puntos / suspensivos" [here intervene the suspension points], objectively separates the subjective statements of "Yo creo" [I believe] and "Yo veo" [I see].

The following section (verses 43-79), which describes the Indian temple, omits completely allusions to writing. The next two sections, however, refer explicitly to the poet's awareness of his activity with introductory and closing parenthetical passages that strongly contrast in their objectives: the first is purposeless and negative ("Escribo sin conocer el desenlace" [I write without knowing the ending]); the second is a moment of fulfillment ("Escribo / Cada letra es un germen" [I write / Each letter is a seed]).

The next section (verses 109-20) parallels lines 43-79 in its description of the holy man and its omission of the poet's awareness of writing. This is followed by a balance between two perceptions, "Todo era igual y todo era distinto" (line 125) [Everything was the same and everything was different], leading into the longest parenthetical phrase (lines 129-38), which in giving the poet's thoughts about the *sadú* could also refer to the poet's feeling of being enclosed in his self-consciousness:

> (Ido ido
> Santo payaso santo mendigo rey maldito
> es lo mismo
>   siempre lo mismo
>   en lo mismo
> Es ser siempre en sí mismo
>   encerrado
> en lo mismo
>   En sí mismo cerrado
> ídolo podrido)
>
> [(Gone   gone
> Saint   clown   saint   beggar   king   damned

```
        it is the same
            always the same
                    within the same
        It is to be always within oneself
                    closed up
        in the same
                In oneself enclosed
        rotted idol)]
```

The use of "ídolo" not only adds to the verbal and rhythmic repetitions, but also provides a link between the echoing "Ido ido" that introduces both this section and the following. In the final section, the poet's experience and his awareness of writing are fused, as they were in the introductory sections. The repetition of "Escribo" and "a la luz de una lámpara" [by the light of a lamp], which are joined here instead of widely separated as in the first sections, recalls the beginning of the poem. But where the writing was questioning before, it is triumphant now ("Sé lo que creo y lo escribo" [I know what I believe and I am writing it]), particularly if the unnamed companion whom he addresses is his poetry ("hablo siempre contigo / hablas siempre conmigo" [I always speak with you / you always speak with me]).

The poem, then, deals with two subjects, the holy man and the poet's writing, which are both separate and interdependent. Both can be seen from either a positive or negative point of view. The sadú's remoteness is either animal or saintly (line 94); he is "desgreñado embadurnado" [disheveled smeared], but his eyes are "un rayo fijo" [stationary lightning]. His refrain "ido ido" [gone gone], can be the echo of ecstasy or of drugs or simply the hunger of a man who is not only a "santo pícaro santo" [holy rogue holy] but also "Santo payaso santo mendigo rey maldito" [Holy clown holy beggar cursed king]. In the same way the poet's effort can be either success or failure: "Todo está y no está" (line 7) [Everything is and is not present]. In verses 30-36 his task is dismissed as names and commonplaces, but nonetheless, he concludes with two emphatic declarations, separated by a doubt: "Yo

creo / aquí intervienen los puntos / suspensivos / Yo veo."
What he believes and what he sees must be determined by the
reader. At the same time, "Yo veo," the last line of the first
section, introduces the following section, in which the poet's
awareness of his writing has no part.

The two subjects are not only joined again in verses 104-26,
but the *sadú* is described by an image, "garabato" (line 88)
[scrawl], that could refer to the writing. The identification, or
the confusion, of the holy man with the poet's struggle for
expression is continued in verses 127-36. The conclusion of
that section, the refrain of "ido ido" in parentheses, is paral-
leled by the last section of the poem, which is introduced by
the refrain without parentheses.

The poet's final judgment of his effort contains the same
ambiguity demonstrated toward the *sadú*. Although the tone
is affirmative and even triumphant, the victory is hollow, for
the poet's grasp of success is transitory. Whether "Los abso-
lutos las eternidades / y sus aledaños" [The absolutes the
eternities / and their outlying areas] are the objects of "escri-
bo" or the subjects of line 146, they are not the poet's theme.
What he finally achieves is a paradox, "Advenimiento del
instante" [Advent of the moment], described in mutually
destructive terms, "el movimiento en que se esculpe / y se
deshace el ser entero" [the movement in which is sculp-
ted / and undone the entire being]. In fact, the poet describes
himself in contradictory terms as both "una historia" and
"Una memoria que se inventa" [A memory that invents
itself], one who speaks with poetry and yet plants symbols in
the dark.

The dual theme is reinforced by the conflicting interpreta-
tions suggested by the arrangements of verses, words, and
phrases, particularly the ambivalent meanings caused by the
absence of punctuation. In line 13, for example, "Corría" [I
ran], standing alone, could logically be a part of the preceding
line ("Entre las casas apagadas" [Among the extinguished
houses]) or of the following ("Entre mis pensamientos encen-
didos" [Among my kindled thoughts]). The lack of commas
and periods enables "Corría" to serve a dual function. At the

same time, this verb constitutes a link between the contrast of "casas apagadas" and "pensamientos encendidos." In the same way, "Yo veo," the concluding verse of that section, is not only the final statement, but also, simultaneously, the introduction to the first verse of the next section, so that the division between the two is both affirmed and denied. Or again, in the concluding section of the poem, the placement in the middle of the line of "no son mi tema" (*Poemas*, 425, line 146) raises doubts about what is being denied, whether "Los absolutos las eternidades / y sus aledaños" or a larger body of verses, perhaps even the entire poem up to this point. The larger rejection is implied by the affirmation, almost immediately, of "Sé lo que creo y lo escribo."

In fact, all the verses that begin in the middle of lines partake of different degrees of ambiguity, depending on which syntactical and logical association the reader chooses to make. The absence of punctuation, therefore, is an invitation to the reader to apply his own pauses and thus to collaborate in the creation of the poem. Although the choices are made with the materials that the poet has supplied and are therefore limited in number, the reader has a vital role in the shaping of both the theme and the elements of the poem that contribute to its definition.

The central placement of verses also contributes to ambivalent metaphors. Does "Jardines serenísimos" (line 16) [most serene gardens], for example, become a metaphor for the stars of the preceding verse or the introduction to "Yo era un árbol" [I was a tree] of the following? Does "Garabato" (line 88) amplify the meaning of "Mono de lo Absoluto" [Ape of the Absolute] or refer to the squatting figure of the *sadú*?

The total effect of contrasts and linking, imagined commas and periods, enjambement, and ambivalent metaphors contributes to opposing interpretations of the entire poem. It can be read as a meaningful or meaningless experience for the poet, who achieves either success or failure in his attempt to convey the significance of the incident. The *sadú* is either a saint and mystic or a dirty and drug-ridden charlatan. The Indian temple, by the same token, is either a lovely shrine or a festering sore of humanity. The poet, in struggling to define the experience, either knows or does not know what he wants to say, and either succeeds or fails in expressing it. These are alternatives that seem to imply a choice, for logically they cannot coexist. For Paz, however, concerned throughout all his poetry with the significance of paradox, they not only coexist but are interdependent. The reader who makes a choice, therefore, misses the fullest significance of the poem, which attempts to fuse opposite poles of experience into a paradoxical unity. A verse in English from another poem of *Ladera este*, "Lectura de John Cage," sums up the poet's intention: "('The situation must be Yes-and-No / not either-or')."

"Tumba del poeta" provides a similar treatment of a similar theme. The conflict (and union) of opposites, the multiplicity of interpretation (both of individual verses and theme), and the involvement of the reader in determining the poem's ultimate significance suggest a pattern that is applicable to all the poems of *Ladera este*.

Unlike "Vrindaban," the subject of the poem is not clearly focused at the outset. The elements of the interior—the book, glass, plant, and record—enumerated without a principal verb, create an abstraction that is at first lacking in coherence. Its timelessness is stressed by "En un allá no sé donde" [In a there I don't know where]. The simplicity of the enumeration digresses in verse 3 with the unusual image involving an adverb modifying a noun ("El verde oscuramente tallo" [The green darkly stalk]). The poem's subject is adumbrated, rather than defined, in verse 6 ("Las cosas anegadas en sus nombres" [Things flooded in their names]), for semantics is only one aspect of language, which is the poet's symbol for the creative process, which is in turn the door to metaphysics.

The first twenty-one verses, in fact, culminating in an exclamation, constitute the introduction. The rapidity of the poet's impressions is emphasized by the "illogical" and synesthetic effects of "Decirlas con los ojos" [To say them with one's eyes] and "Clavarlas" [To fix them], intensified by

"Clavarlo / Como un templo vivo" [Fix it / Like a living temple] and "Plantarlo / Como un árbol" [Plant it / Like a tree]. These verses imply a final revelation of meaning that was previously denied in verse 6. If meaning is lost in names, that is, through language, it must be expressed in another, nonverbal way. The theme of the first section, dramatized by the cry "¡Lenguaje!," is the dilemma of the poet facing the dispersed elements of reality and attempting to join them into a pattern, although he suspects that his medium will fail, or even betray, him.

No sooner is the poem's subject defined as language than the poet gives a succinct illustration of its multiplicity in verses 22 and 23: the stalk and its flower are a metaphor for perception. The expansion of the metaphor here through the repetition of "sol" necessarily draws the reader into multiple possibilities. The most obvious is that the poet vacillates in his choice of a metaphor and decides on "sol"; in this case it is a repetition that has been altered by the intervention of "sexo." Another interpretation joins all three, so that "sol-sexo" equals "sol," suggesting the heat and intensity of the double concept, which could be achieved equally, with a different emphasis, by the verbal equation "sol = sexo = sol." Still another possibility, related to the first, is that the poet has excerpted from an infinite circular repetition of "sol-sexo," so that the reader continues the alternation of "sexo-sol-sexo." Whatever the interpretation, it is supplied by the reader rather than by the text.

A similar multiplicity of experience shapes the last six verses of this section:

> transparencia que sostiene a las cosas
> caídas
>   por la mirada
> leventadas
>   en un reflejo
>   suspendidas

[transparency which sustains things
fallen
          by the glance
lifted
          in a reflection
                    suspended]

The reader's attention is captured by the triple paradox of "caídas," "leventadas," and "suspendidas," balanced by the contradictions of "transparencia," "mirada," and "reflejo." Both series are crossed and separated by the ambiguity of "por la mirada" and "en un reflejo," both of which can be read with either the preceding or the following verse. The typographical arrangement strengthens the total effect of fluidity, which instead of taking final form, is left open by the termination of the section in the concept "suspendidas." Here again the reader must make the final determination.

The progression of the poem from concreteness to abstraction is intensified in the third section, where the references are ambiguous. They may look back to "las cosas" of the previous section or look ahead to the poet's awareness of his writing of the poem, or refer to both subjects. The enumeration of impressions continues, unaided by an independent verb, from lines 35 to 45, with the exception of verse 42. Here the exclamatory "SER" provides a common denominator of verbal significance that retroactively unifies the section and fulfills both the poet's and the reader's yearning for meaning.

Although the second section suggests the poet's success in capturing an elusive meaning, several parallelisms in the concluding sections make one question whether the poem is advancing at all or whether its motion is circular. "En un aquí no sé donde" (line 45) [In a here I don't know where] emphasizes the "allá" [there] of its preceding parallel, verse 27, which is a variation of verse 8. Verse 48 recalls verses 12 and 14. Verse 54 is a reflection of 13. In fact, the final section is a series of restatements and repetitions, including the isolated and emphatic "SER."

The poem's meaning is revealed in the recapitulation of the final section:

                              Un nombre
       comienza
              asirlo plantarlo decirlo
       como un bosque pensante
                              encarnarlo
       Un linaje comienza
                       en un nombre
       un adán
              como un templo vivo
       nombre sin sombra
                       clavado
       como un dios
                 en este aquí sin donde
       ¡Lenguaje!

                              [A name
       begins
              seize it, plant it, say it
       like a forest that thinks
                              flesh it
       A lineage begins
                    in a name
       an adam
              like a living temple
       name without shadow
                       nailed
       like a God
                 in this here-without-where
       Speech!]

The scattered elements of creation enumerated in the first section are presented again, but are given a new meaning, particularly through the philosophical pun of *nombre/ hombre*. "Un nombre / comienza" [A name / begins], therefore, equates man and language. Although the same efforts of seizing, planting, and saying are described, they are now successful, and are carried to the higher level of "encarnarlo." The lasting significance of poetic expression is implied by the verse immediately following the incarnation, "Un linaje comienza," and by the explicit reference to "un nombre / un adán," in which the small letter indicates the general category of *nombre/hombre*.

In the recapitulation the order of subjects (*templo - árbol - dios* [temple - tree - god]) has been modified (*bosque - adán - dios* [forest - adam - god]). The result is the recognition of fulfillment in the present ("En este aquí sin donde," line 58), so that the exclamation of "¡Lenguaje!" represents a cry of success rather than the frustration or longing of line 21. In that sense, verses 60 and 61 could well be the conclusion of the poem as the poet happily observes the annihilation of his subjectivity in the inception of the poem, in the kind of paradox used often by mystics. The poem could end equally in either of the two subsequent verses, which could also be interpreted as postscripts or echoes of the conclusion.

In the penultimate verse ("sombra de un nombre instantáneo" [shadow of an instantaneous name]), however, Paz projects a new dimension for the poem. In the two previous references to the flower without a shadow and the name without a shadow, Paz refers to the real meaning of life unobscured by language, to an ideal world that is just the opposite of the poem's point of departure, "las cosas anegadas en sus nombres." In this case, the shadow represents a return to a clouded reality, to confusion, and to obscurity, negating the felicitous resolution of the three preceding verses. The shadow, moreover, is not only that of language, but, because of the pun of *nombre/hombre*, of the poet himself, who both in his presence and his use of language is irremediably transitory.

The poem could also have ended with the negative impact of verse 64. However, as if unwilling to adopt either a positive or negative point of view, the poet chooses instead to stress the ambiguity of the poem and the dual nature of his dilemma. In stating so flatly that he will never know his (that is, the poem's) outcome, Paz asserts an existential paradox of affirmation and denial, fulfillment and limitation, and poetic success and failure. The conclusion that is inconclusive is a self-contained contradiction that makes the poem open-ended. At the same time, it provides an epitaph for the poet that justifies the poem's title.

Both of these poems deal essentially with the same subject, the difficulties of the poet in defining reality through the act of writing. The fact that both seem to end inconclusively suggests the cyclical nature of the poet's thought, as well as of the poems. His goal in both cases is the Buddhist stage of enlightenment in which dualities disappear. The essence he seeks is the mystical experience that merges perception with reality, so that language is no longer separate from the experience it describes. In these poems and throughout *Ladera este*, the intention is to break the dichotomy between the poem and its subject. Paradoxically, the success of the poem would abolish the poem.

The dominant feature of "Viento entero" is the use of one of the poet's favorite devices, the paradox, as a refrain.[2] The short, symbolic, and philosophical commentary, "El presente es perpetuo," not only divides the poem into seven approximately equal sections of nineteen to twenty-five verses each, plus two shorter closing sections of seventeen and fifteen verses, but also contains the key to the poem's theme.

The first section (lines 1-19) provides the geographical background against which the poem takes place. Its development of contrasts, particularly between the eternity of the mountains and the transitory nature of the bazaar, serves as the introduction to the poem. Other contrasts, between light and sound ("Molino de sonidos / El bazar tornasolea" [A mill of sounds / The bazaar gleams]) and between spirituality and reality (the "príncipes en harapos" [princes in rags] who "rezan orinan meditan" [pray urinate meditate]) recall the similarly mixed portrait of the *sadú* in "Vrindaban," and suggest a fundamental duality, both in life and in the poet's vision, that shapes the entire composition. At the same time,

the tone of the introductory section is impeccably imper-
sonal. Not only is "yo" lacking, but also any person to whom
the reader feels any relationship or even interest. The traders
of the bazaar and their children are presented with the life-
lessness of picture postcards. They fit into the detached de-
scription at the same level, and with the same lack of
affective reactions, as the enumeration of sounds.

The vivid contrast between the first and second sections is
introduced by the dramatic action of the day's leap through
the floodgates of the year. Without any transition, the girl
presented on Parisian streets seems to be a capricious change
of subject. But when the poet takes her by the hand through
"los cuatro espacios los tres tiempos" [the four spaces the
three times], they return to the day of beginning, which the
reader recognizes is the day of verse 21 and also June 21.
Although the girl's significance is vague, although causality
does not exist in this section, time has made a circle.

In the third section (lines 44-68), the time, place, and
people are explicitly identified in the scene in the poet's
garden. Parallel to the "illogical" appearance of the girl in the
second section is the introduction (through "Un gran vuelo
de cuervos" [A great flight of crows], which could refer either
to part of the garden scene or to the soldiers of the following
scene or both) of ideological conflicts, one concerning a cur-
rent event in Santo Domingo, the other religious violence
during the English conquest of India. The concluding symbol
of the section is enigmatic, but seems to suggest that the
builders of modern Mexico will be both visible and vulnera-
ble in their transparent cathedrals and pyramids.

The fourth section (lines 69-91) returns to the subject of
the beloved introduced in the third. The erotic combination
of sun, nudity, and the red bedspread is developed. In a process
of free association, she is *fruta* and *dátil* [date] which calls to
mind Datia, an abandoned fortress whose symmetry,
according to the poet's notes, symbolizes a solipsism. The
identification of the beloved with the girl in Paris is under-
scored by the repetition or recasting of verses: 88 is a varia-
tion of 29, as 90 (with the precision of the definite article)

restates 35. The symbolism of the world's transparency, suggesting an underlying unity to diverse appearances, applies equally to the beloved, described as a diaphanous drop, and to the "real" girl. Furthermore, this symbolism is stressed by its climactic position at the end of this section, immediately preceding the statement of the refrain.

The fifth section is clearly, almost harshly, divided into parts that seem completely unrelated. Verses 92-105 describe the austerity of a dramatic and cruel landscape that is softened only by the reference to water (line 103), shortly personified as the beloved's eyes, "tus ojos de agua humana." This introduces an erotic passage that although certainly not unprecedented in the poet's work, is more explicit than most. Only the refrain at the beginning of the next section separates the lovers' passion from the hermit who keeps vigil at the tomb of a saint.

Looking at the fifth and sixth sections together, it is difficult to say whether passion intrudes on a description of the landscape or vice versa. Although the torrent of verse 121 recalls the "desfiladero" [mountain pass], "ola" [wave], "salto" [waterfall], and "espuma" [foam] that shortly before symbolized their union, the beloved's repetition of the poet's name is, and yet somehow is not, the same. In the same way the landscape participates in, and yet is apart from, the scene of love. The poet's attempt to grasp meaning from archeological remains blends with his attempt to find order in language, which is based in turn on his oath to be the earth and wind over her bones. Love and the landscape have merged, at least in these verses. One could say, in fact, that they have merged in both the present and perpetual times of the refrain.

The seventh section (lines 143-64) at first glance seems to be so fragmented that it lacks unity. The scattered personal observations of reality, many cast in surrealistic imagery, reflect the poet's random thoughts, perhaps as he is falling asleep. On closer inspection, however, one can see a dual subject similar to that of the preceding section: the first half (lines 143-52) deals with the outer world, extending as far as the concept of the universe; the second half deals with the sleeping woman. Line 156, "Espacio espacios animados," apparently unrelated to the rest of the second half, becomes clearer when the concept of space reoccurs and symbolically connects woman with the universe and the refrain:

> madre de las razas errantes
> >   de soles y de hombres
> Emigran los espacios
> >   el presente es perpetuo
> >   [lines 161-65]

> [mother of wandering races
> >   of suns and men
> Spaces migrate
> >   the present is perpetual]

The fertility of "Anima mundi," emphatically developed by two appositions ("materia maternal" and "madre de las razas errantes"), is contradicted by the sterility of verse 160.

Verse 156, furthermore, contains an internal contradiction as the poet retains both the singular and the plural of "espacio" and qualifies the plural with "animados." By means of a grammatical impossibility, he conveys dramatically the changing forms of meaning: the sleeping woman at the same time is a symbol of life for him and of numerous perceptions outside his vision.

The eighth section (lines 165-81) is unified by the concept of time as endless and therefore meaningless. For both the gods and mankind, time is the same headlong fall into space. The random view of the barefoot child near Lahor is, because of this concept of time, both insignificant and symbolic. In the same way, and for the same reason, opposites are reconciled: life and death, heaven and earth. The concluding verses of this section, leading again to the central contradiction of the refrain, imply that it really makes no difference whether the vision of the poplars is ascending or descending, for both are the same, or perhaps both are partial—and erroneous—views of the same reality:

Entre el cielo y la terra suspendidos
unos cuantos álamos
vibrar de luz más que vaivén de hojas
                                    ¿suben o bajan?
[Between sky and earth suspended
a group of poplars
quivering of light more than trembling of leaves
                                    do they rise or fall?]

In the concluding section (lines 182-97) the poet's
awareness of his experience, and particularly of love, is re-
lated to all of his previous life, just as this section suggests a
relationship to the entire poem. The beloved who reconciles
the opposites of fire and water recalls the previous statements
of the same contradiction in verses 29, 88, and 188. In com-
parison to the vision of the world in which opposites are
harmonious, reality is meaningless (192). The implication of
line 193 is that it is, and yet is not, the same day, for time has
lost its normal form, as has the world and the poet's con-
templation of it. The last verse, with its emotional separation
of "cuerpos / Tendidos" [bodies / Extended] sums up the
transcendent effects of love.

The theme of "Viento entero," and the influence on Paz of
Buddhism, are indicated by the relationship of *sunyata* to
samsara [reality] in his note to the poem:

> *Sunyata* es un término que designa el concepto central
> del budismo madhyamika: la vacuidad absoluta. Un
> relativismo radical: todo es relativo e impermanente,
> sin excluir a la afirmación sobre la relatividad e imper-
> manencia del mundo. La proposición que niega la reali-
> dad también se disuelve y así la negación del mundo por
> la crítica es asimismo su recuperación: *Samsara* es *Nir-*
> *vana* porque todo es *sunyata.*
>
>   [*Poemas*, 690]

[*Sunyata* is a term that designates the central concept of
Madhyamika Buddhism: absolute emptiness. A radical

relativism: everything is relative and impermanent, including the affirmation concerning the relativity and impermanence of the world. The proposition that denies reality also dissolves itself and thus the negation of the world through critical inquiry is also its recovery: *Samsara* is *Nirvana* because everything is *sunyata.*]

"Viento entero" has a dual subject, the poet's vision of reality and woman's place in it. The world can be seen as meaningful or meaningless. At times the reader may feel that it is both simultaneously. In the same manner love is either permanent and significant or transitory and commonplace. Even more significant is the relationship between love and reality; the definition of one affects the character of the other. The poet, unable to assign fixed categories to his perceptions, shares his uncertainty with the reader.

A more extensive influence of Buddhism is apparent in "Lectura de John Cage."[3] In his note to this poem Paz openly outlines its theme:

> En la literatura budista Mahayana, especialmente en la tántrica, se repite una y otra vez la fórmula *Samsara es Nirvana, Nirvana es Samsara.* Es una expresión que condensa una de las ideas cardinales de la tendencia madhyamika: la identidad última entre la realidad fenomenal (Samsara: el ciclo del deseo ignorante de sí y de sus reincarnaciones) y la transcendental (Nirvana: un estado de beatitud indefinible excepto por la negación: no es esto ni aquello). Samsara y Nirvana son equivalentes porque ambos son modos de la vacuidad y el verdadero sabio trasciende su aparente dualidad. Pero el poema dice algo ligeramente distinto.
>
> [*Poemas*, 689]

> [In Mahayana Buddhist literature, especially in Tantric literature, the formula "Samsara is Nirvana, Nirvana is Samsara" is repeated again and again. It is an expression that condenses one of the cardinal ideas of Madhyamika thought: the ultimate identity between phenomenal

reality (Samsara: the cycle of desire ignorant of itself
and of its reincarnations) and the transcendental (Nir-
vana: a state of beatitude indefinable except through
negation: it is neither this nor that). Samsara and Nir-
vana are equivalent because both are modes of emp-
tiness and the true wise man transcends their apparent
duality. But the poem says something somewhat dif-
ferent.]

The final sentence above is a masterful understatement, de-
signed to draw the reader into a closer examination of the
poem. In fact, "Lectura de John Cage" contradicts the equiv-
alence of *samsara* and *nirvana*.

The title of this poem suggests a choice that must be
made among numerous, perhaps limitless, interpretations of
Cage's meaning. The first forty verses, terminating with
"Silencio es música / música no es silencio," key verses
which are repeated later in the poem, constitute the begin-
ning of a definition of what we take for reality, which is the
closest translation of *samsara*. Characteristically for Paz, the
approach is made in terms of the opposition of the first two
verses of one word each, just as Cage's first statement,
"Music without measurements," is a paradox in conven-
tional music and just as his second statement suggests an
unconventional mixture of sound with circumstances,
which are traditionally, at least in part, visual. Verses 5-8
develop the interlocking dualities of inner-outer and seeing-
hearing. Verse 9 implies that the origin of music is external if
the poet is the circumstance through which it passes. If verse
11 is a restatement of 5-6, verse 12 converts the duality of
identity of verses 7-8 to a dual perception of one phe-
nomenon. These conflicting dualities suggest a reality
beyond the conflicts, perceived intuitively, although nega-
tively, in the quotation from Duchamp in verse 13. In verses
14-18 the poet attempts to reconcile his limited, partial, sub-
jective, and defective perception with the universal harmony
glimpsed by Cage in verses 19-20.

The remainder of this section develops the precept an-

nounced in verses 21-22, which defines silence as the ulti-
mate expression of music, just as the aim of architecture is
the comprehension of space. The differentiation between the
two (verses 30-36) is crucial: silence is an extension and final
development of music, but music, as movement, is not a part
of silence. The concluding statement, whose consequences
are not fully developed in the following section, contradicts
the equivalence of *samsara* and *nirvana* asserted in Paz's note
above.

The second section (verses 41-67) builds its philosophical
edifice on the foundation of the first: enlightenment includes
reality, but reality is not enlightenment. The paradox stated
in verse 43 leads to ignorance, the abolition of comprehen-
sion, which is the ultimate understanding. Beginning with
the awareness of phenomena that seems to be an absolute
("Oír los pasos de esta tarde" [To hear these afternoon
footsteps]), the poet finds a deeper awareness in actually
seeing the afternoon (verse 50). In both states, he is ex-
emplifying the general perceptions of verses 11 and 12. Even
more important is the fact that the ultimate reality of the
afternoon seen here becomes, in turn, invisible in the last
verse of the poem.

The quotation from Cage ("Let our life obscure / The dif-
ference between art and life") calls to mind the analogy
between music and words, anticipated by the first two verses
of the poem, "Leído / Desleído" [Read / Unread]. This analo-
gy, supported by Paz's constant explicit and implicit concern
for the meaning of language, contributes to the comprehen-
sion of "Lectura de John Cage." Although silence lacks sig-
nificance and significance has no silence, there is a music
(that is, a poem) that joins the two. It is, then, the poem that
confers ultimate meaning on nothingness.

The fact that the poet has returned to the subjects of music
and silence, which opened and closed the introductory sec-
tion, gives a circular structure to the poem's development.
Here, as in other repetitions, the reader perceives the lines as
more meaningful because of their restatement. In this case,
the references to silence and music have been strengthened

by two repetitions immediately preceding: verse 55 restates 39 as 58 restates 40.

In the third section (verses 68-102) Paz illustrates through concrete examples the relationship between silence and music. There is, first, a distiction between different kinds of silence: that of his room (verse 68) is not absolute if it contains the sound of his body, which contains, at a level more remote from the poet's perception, unspoken thoughts. The afternoon, previously used as an example of different kinds of perception (verses 44-51), both stops and advances, and this paradox is seen both in isolation and as a background for the sound of male and female bodies calling to each other. That dialogue is given as the example of music without notes.

If music is real (perceivable) and silence is an idea (abstraction), Paz wonders how he should classify John Cage, and becomes lost in his metaphor. Cage, he states, is Japanese, meaning that his creation is closer to Japan than to America. He is like sun on snow (the symbolism of the Japanese flag?), two elements that cannot be the same but whose relationship is so close that they cannot be distinguished, not even in negative terms (verse 87). The isolated "O" (verse 86) graphically symbolizes the sun and introduces two additional contradictions: Cage is American and not American. The sun-snow paradox is intermingled with that of silence-music in the last four verses before the quotation from Cage (verses 101-2) that concludes this section: one category need not exclude another, but becomes part of it.

The dramatization of this concept (verses 103-16) constitutes the poem's conclusion:

                    Entre el silencio y la música,
                                                el arte y la vida,
                    la nieve y el sol
                                    hay un hombre.
                    Ese hombre es John Cage
                                        (committed
                    to the nothing in between).

                                        Dice una palabra:
    no nieve no sol,
                    una palabra
    que no es
            silencio:
    A year from Monday you will hear it.

    La tarde se ha vuelto invisible.

    [Between silence and music
                        art and life
    snow and sun
                    there is a man
    This man is John Cage
                    (*committed*
    to the nothing in between).
                        He says a word
    not snow not sun
                    a word
    which is not
            silence:
    A year from Monday you will hear it.

    The afternoon has become invisible.]

Cage's words are neither sun nor snow, neither silence nor music, but the bridge between concepts. In the contemplation of this mystery, reality, as we normally think of it, vanishes. The isolated last verse, the climax of the poem, marks the disappearance of the philosophical basis for the poet's perceptions, the afternoon itself. The implication is that the poet has left it behind for a new stage of consciousness beyond the expressive powers of the poem. He has entered, as does the reader finishing the poem, a silence that is different from that with which the poem began, if only because both the poet and the reader have been trying to find the reality beyond silence.

   If there is a single characteristic that joins all of the poems of *Ladera este*, it is the intense desire to define a reality beyond appearances and perception, the attempt to reach "the other shore" that is integral to all of Paz's poetry. What is unique here is the expansion of this theme into the dominant objective of this book, so that it permeates all of the poems. They become, essentially, glosses on this theme. The poet's philosophical mysticism, if we may use this term to indicate a nonreligious aspiration to transcend reality, clearly has been expanded through his contact with Buddhist, and particularly Tantric, thought during his lengthy stay in India. Tantra, which defies definition as a religion or way of thought is an activist cult that cuts across both Hinduism and Buddhism: "Tantra, in fact, plunges one back into the roots of one's own identity, not just by discussing social roles and interpersonal communication, and not by offering the kind of clear-cut or comforting answers given by the dogmatic theology of straight religions. Tantra says 'If you do these things which Tantrikas have discovered, you will find yourself in a position to experience what the truth is about yourself and your world, as directly as you can experience the street.' "[4] Tantra concentrates on the question of time, locating its origin not outside man, but within the psychophysical organism operating through each individual.[5] Seen in these terms, Paz's refrain "El presente es perpetuo" applies to all of the poems in *Ladera este*.

Equally important in this book, and as extensively used as the development of themes of time and reality, is the significance of sexuality: "The act of continuous creation is expressed by patterns of sexual activity, which is seen as infused with a sense of totally transcendent love. The existence of the world is thought of as a continuous giving birth by the yoni (vulva) of the female principle resulting from a continuous infusion of the seed of the male, in sexual delight."[6] In the philosophical context of Tantra, then, the eroticism of many of the poems here is more than a praise of love; it is related to a concept of existence, to the fullest awareness of life, and to the attempt to reach the other shore of existence. The act of love is a *mantra*, a mystic exercise, through which the essence of life is perceived.

The demands which Paz makes on his reader in this volume are greater than those of his previous work. The goal, a reality beyond language, is not attainable within the poem itself; if the reader glimpses it, he does so only after leaving the springboard provided by the poem. In fact, since the experience is not conveyed by words, the poet cannot even share his experience with others, but can only provide the framework within which his experience takes place, in the hope that it can be replicated by his readers.

The risks of this kind of poetry are obvious. The mystical approach to a nonreligious goal is not fashionable now, and probably never has been in Hispanic poetry. Unless the reader is made to share the objective, he may feel, as some of Paz's contemporaries do, that the poet is simply playing with words and concepts. Many readers may be stranded on this shore, unable to visualize the other, or even confused about the purpose of the bridge.[7] The demands on the reader of *Ladera este* have expanded those required for *Piedra de sol.* In *Piedra de sol*, the circularity of the poem obliges the reader to evaluate the experience he has just had, and by contrasting the different effects produced by the identical verses of the beginning and the end, to define the theme of the poem. To oversimplify the approach, we may say that the reader transcends reality by repeating it. In *Ladera este*, on the other hand, he is given the opportunity for transcendence by the manner in which the poem invites, rather than dictates, a metaphysical journey.

"Contigo" ["With You"] illustrates the ways in which these demands are formulated, and is a paradigm for all of the poems in the book:

> Ráfagas turquesa
> loros fugaces en parejas
>   Vehemencias
> el mundo llamea
>   Un árbol
> hirviente de cuervos
> arde sin quemarse

                        Quieta
            entre los altos tornasoles
                                    eres
            una pausa de la luz
                        El día
            es una gran palabra clara
            palpitación de vocales
                            Tus pechos
            maduran bajo mis ojos
                            Mi pensamiento
            es más ligero que el aire
                            Soy real
            veo mi vida y mi muerte
            El mundo es verdadero
            Veo
                habito una transparencia

            [Gusts of wind turquoise
            parrots fleeing in pairs
                            Vehemences
            the world flames
                        A tree
            seething with crows
            blazes without burning
                            Quiet
            among the fall sunflowers
                                    you are
            a pause of the light
                            The day
            is a great clear word
            palpitation of vowels
                            Your breasts
            ripen under my eyes
                            My thought
            is lighter than the air
                            I am real
            I see my life and my death

The world is true
I see
I inhabit a transparency]

Its main elements, which have already been discussed in the longer poems analyzed here, are landscape (the world), woman (love), and reality (meaning). In fact, this brief composition of 23 verses is precisely divided into three equal parts, one for each of the subjects. Within the format of two columns that is typical of this volume, the right column presents a condensed version of the poem, distilling in its eight verses of one and two words each the essence of the theme. They provide a shorthand comprehension of the poem through the effective use of five nouns, two descriptive adjectives, and two forms of the verb *ser*.

The two right-column concepts, "Vehemencias" and "Un árbol," recreate the effect of the longer, left-column verses (1, 2, 4, 6 and 7), which suggest the noise and flaming colors that wound the senses of the observer of the parrots and crows. Quietly, in the center of the day (and of the poem), the beloved is both a hiatus in the light and a word that brings order to sound. "Tus pechos / maduran bajo mis ojos" indicates how desire not only transforms its object but gives meaning to it.

The effect of love on the poet, introduced by the subjective phrase "Mi pensamiento" in the concluding section, has transformed the world of the first part, but in terms that give meaning to reality: "Soy real," which is the final statement and climax of the right column, implies that only now, and for the first time, does the poet recognize himself. Not only is he fully realized, but, we are told in the four remaining left-column verses, he perceives the meaning of life and death and the world. For the first time, "Veo" suggests, he truly sees. The meaning of the final verse is ecstatic: all of reality has become transparent as he looks through it to a meaning outside of it. In this simple, brief, and deeply felt poem, whose subject is a commonplace in poetry of all languages, Paz has summarized the approach, the themes, and the technique of all of *Ladera este*.

6 *Pasado en claro*
The Poem Itself

Soy la sombra que arrojan mis palabras

[I am the shadow my words cast]

—Paz, *Pasado en claro*

The hiatus of six years between the publication of *Ladera este* (1969) and *Pasado en claro* (1975) constitutes the longest interruption in Paz's poetic production if one discounts the somewhat whimsical ideograms of *Topoemas* and *Renga*, of which he was one of four authors. This period of germination yielded a long poem that marks a simplification of structure within the poet's trajectory. From multiple relationships and polarities, his approach is reduced to the single plane of autobiography. The complexity of the poem is achieved not through its structure or its diction (which is a return to the simplicity of *Piedra de sol*), but through its theme and the reader's application of it to his own life.

Like *Piedra de sol* and *Blanco*, *Pasado en claro* attempts to summarize the poet's view of himself and also of the world and of his relationship to it. Each is defined in terms of the others in the three poems. What differentiates *Pasado en claro* from its predecessors is not only the emphasis placed on internal reality, but also what we may call the direction of the poem. Both *Piedra de sol* and *Blanco* open outward, proceeding from internal to external meaning. *Pasado en claro*, on the other hand, reverses the philosophical trajectory. Once the relationship between the self and the world is established, the poem turns constantly inward in its quest for values, order, and significance.

The most helpful studies of *Pasado en claro*, by Liscano, Gimferrer, and Oviedo, reach similar conclusions through different reactions to the poem. Liscano sees it as a "poema existencial de honda indagación ontológica y lúcida intensidad reflexiva" [existential poem of profound ontological inquiry and lucid philosophical intensity]. Its broad purpose is nothing less than a duplication of the cosmos. Although the work begins and ends as a meditation on time, memory, and their connection with the present, three other subjects are significant: language and time, language and memory, and language in itself. The structure of the poem, which in its circularity seems similar to *Piedra de sol*, is actually that of a sphere. Almost exactly in the center of the poem is the depiction of a primordial fig tree, which symbolizes the illumination of the poet.[1]

Gimferrer, too, sees the structure of the poem as circular, proceeding, like *Blanco*, from silence to silence, or rather from—and to—the imminence of the word. Like Liscano, he stresses the central role of language. The complex relationships among writing, the word, the world, and awareness are impossible to analyze separately because each unfolds and generates other meanings. The poem resolves the duality between time and permanence through a glimpse of transcendence: although we are enclosed by words, there exists another area beyond them that is an ultimate reality. Paradoxically, Paz shows us through language a form of knowledge outside it, but that vision too is temporary.[2]

Oviedo does not hesitate to classify *Pasado en claro* as Paz's most important poem in a decade, and also the most confessional and moving. In its response to the question of identity presented by "yo" (who should not be confused with the poet), the poem is an anagnorisis, a self-recognition. The procedure through which this recognition is developed is "a la vez doloroso y paliativo, lento y urgente, oscuro y lúcido" [at the same time painful and palliative, slow and urgent, obscure and lucid]. The entire text is an arrow which the poet shoots at his own center. This is the subject of the poem, in spite of its narrative tone. The pattern, based on two triads of opposites (air-fire, water-earth, and darkness-light, which are contained in, and transcended by, reality-writing, memory-present, and passion-knowledge), is a hexagram.[3]

The title, like those of the other major poems, invites

ambiguous interpretations. In *Piedra de sol* the reference is either to the Aztec calendar stone or to the fusion of sun and stone that liberates the poet at the poem's conclusion to begin the cycle again in the introductory verses. *Blanco* signifies both the space to be filled by the reader (as well as by the poet) and the target at which thought and feeling are aimed. In both poems the ambiguities are complementary rather than exclusive, so that the different interpretations reinforce each other and add to the reader's awareness of the poem's breadth. *Pasado en claro*, however, as several critics have noted, rests on opposing interpretations. One is that the poet's past is now seen with clarity, so that the result of his review is not to change the facts but to see at last their real significance. The other is based on the idiomatic use of the term as revision, which suggests that the poet does not recall his past but rewrites it. The assumption of the latter interpretation is that the past is not recapturable, and that one can only reshape past experiences in terms of present perceptions. In that sense there is no personal history but a series of histories, each depending on a different set of circumstances. An additional meaning denotes insomnia. The title, therefore, is contradictory. The impossibility of conveying several meanings in English resulted in the interesting but quite different title of the translation, *A Draft of Shadows*.

The revised poem consists of 19 sections of 605 verses of 7, 9, 11, and 19 syllables.[4] Recollections of his childhood and early adolescence are mingled with Paz's awareness of current experience, particularly the writing of the poem. The temporal limitation of the subject excludes one of the poet's constant themes, the perception of the world through erotic love, which has come to be one of his trademarks. So pervasive is that theme in Paz's work that its absence here constitutes a change in his poetic itinerary.

Equally dramatic is the full development of the confessional voice, with its emphasis on autobiographical elements and psychological self-awareness. There are, certainly, a number of antecedents in Paz's poetry for this, as Oviedo notes. In addition to the autobiographical reminiscences of

Piedra de sol, grouped at the symbolic and structural center of the poem, Oviedo cites the much earlier references of separate poems in *Libertad bajo palabra,* particularly "Cuarto de hotel," "Elegía interrumpida," "El ausente," and selections from *¿Aguila o sol?.* The most important antecedent is "¿No hay salida?" of *La estación violenta.*[5]

It is significant that the chronological gap between the publication of that collection (1958) and *Pasado en claro* is twenty-seven years, during which Paz generally excluded autobiographical themes from his poetry. This is not to say that he omits references to events and people, but that he does not utilize them to study his own development retrospectively. Yet his awareness of their importance for his understanding of who he is and what he represents is conveyed often in numerous candid interviews and in his collaboration with an early biographer.[6] In *Pasado en claro,* therefore, he takes up a subject that was only fragmentary in his earlier poetry and that was put aside for more than a quarter of a century, elevates it to a philosophical level, and attempts to understand the world through self-awareness.

After the epigraph's definition of the poem's subject as childhood, the opening eight verses intensively develop a series of interlocking abstractions. Their subject, the "pasos mentales" [footsteps in the mind], is defined paradoxically as the poet balances two unsatisfactory approximations, poised between thought and feeling. Their unsubstantiality is intensified by locating them among the memory's echoes; by the opposition of "inventa y borra" [invents and erases], linked by the colon to the paradox of "sin caminar caminan" [without walking they walk]; and by the image of the journey's goal as a present time that is a hanging bridge between letters, dramatized by the enjambment of "puente tendido" [bridge slung]. The introductory verses convey an atmosphere of movement, fluidity, and change in which the poem will develop. Verses 9-11 again attempt to define the footsteps, which also vanish into air. Verses 12-13 are not an abandonment of meaning but an identification of its hiding place.

The contrast between the first thirteen and the final seven

verses of this section is marked by the image of devastating
sunlight that razes the shadowy landscape and opens the
poet's forehead. It is interesting to note that this curious
image is the culminating one of *Piedra de sol*, representing
the climactic end of the poet's journey before he resumes the
circular path that is simultaneously the conclusion and in-
troduction of that poem. Here the sun is used as the begin-
ning rather than the end of the journey, disclosing the
immense space within the poet.

The final sentence has two unusual features that reinforce
its function as the climax of the first section. The two adverbs
that constitute verse 16 have three distinct interpretations: as
joint modifiers of either the preceding verb "arrasa" [razes] or
the following verb "amaneciendo" [as they dawn], or as sepa-
rate modifiers with the closest adverb modifying each of the
verbs. In the latter case, of course, a comma would normally
divide the two. The fact that the poet has avoided punctua-
tion here is an indication of the same encouragement of
ambivalent readings that figures prominently in *Ladera este*.
Equally interesting in the same sentence is the typographical
arrangement of verse 19, which projects to the right in isola-
tion to suggest in its form the balcony over the precipice that
it describes. Paz cannot be described as a writer of concrete
poetry, but he clearly is acquainted with one of its main
techniques.

Although the theme of language does not have a major role
in the first section, the repeated references to it adumbrate its
general importance in the poem. The "puente / tendido en-
tre una letra y otra" [bridge / slung from one letter to the
next], the reference to the pause between two words, and
most significant, the sun's destruction of "los escombros / de
lo que digo" [the rubble / of what I am saying] suggest the
intimate connection between the mysterious footsteps and
the language in which the poet attempts to define them. The
words that are used, and the poet's awareness of the writing
process, will form part of the quest that the entire poem
represents.

Foreshadowing the technique used to join many of the

sections of the poem, the concept of self ("balcón al voladero / dentro de mí [balcony / perched within me]) serves as a transition to the introductory verse of the following section ("Me alejo de mí mismo" [I drift away from myself]), which at the same time initiates a movement away from the self. This movement abruptly reverses itself—"voy al encuentro de mí mismo" (II,20) [I travel toward myself]—in a contradiction that underscores the shifting views of realities that constitute his vision.

The "pasos" and the repetition of "caminar" in the introductory section combine with the "Me alejo" and "senda" [path] of the second section's first verses to announce the beginning of the poet's quest. In another linking with the first section, verse 9 ("desde mi frente salgo a un mediodía" [from my forehead I set out toward a noon]) is the sequel to I,18 ("el sol abre mi frente" [the sun opens my forehead]). The intervening verses take up the first section's concern with language, which will reappear not only in this section, but, significantly, throughout the poem. That the search for meaning in language is as arduous as the search for reality is indicated by verse 3 ("senda de piedra y de cabras" [this path of rocks and goats]), which recalls "un puñado de cabras es un rebaño de piedras" [a handful of goats is a herd of stones] in "Himno entre ruinas."

If the poet's intention is to outline a quest for meaning through memory, it is not surprising that he should begin with the obvious fragmentation of subject in the second section. From an initial reflection on writing, the poet describes a moment of keen awareness and then an abandoned patio. In spite of certain details—the ash tree, the adobe, the mushroom, and the newt—the patio seems not only insubstantial but changeable. It is "Ni allá ni aquí: por esa linde / de duda" [Neither here nor there: through that frontier / of doubt]; the ash tree is an "aparición," conveying both of the very different meanings conveyed by this term. The patio is "inconclusivo," threatened by the uncertainties of writing. The walls that surround it are, paradoxically, between being and nonbeing. Since no conclusions are possible about the patio's existence or its continuity, the poet implies that it exists only in his imagination at the moment he is writing the poem. The fluid creation of the patio, which is presented more as a mirage than a reality, derives from the poet's consciousness of himself in the act of creating it, admirably depicted in the first eight verses of the second section. The act of writing, "sus raíces de tinta en el subsuelo del lenguaje" [sinking its ink roots in the subsoil of language], suggests that the poet has through his effort made contact with one of the basic forces of life, which is limitless and timeless. The poet, seeing himself in the act of creation, becomes both agent and object in the lines "Ando entre las imágenes de un ojo / desmemoriado. Soy una de sus imágenes" (II,29-30) [I walk among the images / of an eye that has lost its memory. / I am one of its images], and reshapes the same thought, now in terms of a child falling in a well, as the section's conclusion. The contradictory nature of his creation is developed through the multiple paradoxes and repetitions of the final seven verses, both in meaning and in form, particularly "el pozo de la cuenta de mi cuento" (II,45) [the well of the account of my account]. The final suggestion here, that of the poet's own unsubstantiality, his shadow, underlines the need of an ultimate reality.

Oviedo's perceptive observation of the use of three elemental pairs, air-fire, water-earth, and darkness-light, is particularly applicable to the linked subjects of the second and third sections.[7] The Baroque image of the liquid ash tree foreshadows the dominant image of the well at the section's conclusion, which flows into the lagoon at the beginning of section III. Almost in the center of this section, beginning with verse 14, the imagery shifts abruptly from water to fire, which dominates the rest of this section. The change in imagery underscores the equally abrupt transition of subject: from a pre-Columbian lagoon, the site of Tenochtitlán, to the poet's library glowing in the setting sun. The final five verses of this section are a coda on writing, which now eclipses the lagoon. Its function here is just the opposite of the first section's reflection on writing that served as an introduction to deeper exploration of reality. Here it negates the previous reality, closing the door of inquiry. Nonetheless, a new reality is implied by "cuchicheos" [whispers] from the jungle of letters. There is a form of life hidden from the poet's vision.

All of the fourth section is in effect a denial that any progress has been made in the definition of reality. The clouded mirror of memory cannot reflect any image. The implication of the poet's question about where he has been suggests that he has not been anywhere. Since reality is perceived only through words, there is none outside of them. If "Ver al mundo es deletrearlo" [To see the world is to spell it], it follows that articulating language is a way (the only way?) of reaching reality. But if the words are at the bottom of "las aguas turbias de ese charco" [the troubled waters of that pool], which is dried by the sun's heat, what stability does the poet's past have? The repetition in the last verse of "¿Dónde estuve?" (Where was I?), which introduced the section in verse 2 and marked its center in verse 13, stresses the need to begin the quest again.

The fifth section begins with a response to the closing question of the fourth that is an unconclusive answer: "Yo estoy en donde estuve." Oviedo expresses well the intimate relationship between memory and the poet's consciousness: "El yo percibe que el pasado realmente no *existió:* más bien *existe* como una recreación persistente de la imaginación. El tiempo, por lo tanto, es una ilusión; ayer está aquí y estará mañana. Todos los pasados son uno[8] [The "I" perceives that the past really *did not exist:* rather it *exists* as a persistent re-creation of the imagination. Time, therefore, is an illusion; yesterday is here and will be tomorrow. All past times are one]. What contrasts with the subject of the preceding sections, however, is the poet's choice and development of a symbolic memory, the primordial fig tree. Verses 3 to 6 succinctly define the timeless world of the tree, in which diverse historical periods, events, and people, including the poet's childhood companions, are equated. In its magic center, reality acquires a meaning that is lacking in life outside. Eroticism is the coat of arms over the entrance to a magical world.

The sixth section comprises a litany to this timeless world, with six subsections introduced by the phrase "allá dentro" and a seventh, longer than the others, by the verse "no hay escuela allá dentro" [there is no school there, inside]. These are variations on the fig tree's magic, expressed in the pervasiveness of green (seen in the tides, blood, and fire of verses 31-35), the multiple synesthesias of the second subsection (verses 36-38), the merging of light, water, and time (verses 55-56), and the beatific vision of a timeless world in which opposites coexist (verses 64-70). The common denominator for all these magical changes is a sense of order and purpose and a tone of fulfillment. The section's three concluding verses clearly suggest knowledge, particularly self-knowledge, and communication in a language that is universal.

The seventh section is an illustration of the theme announced by its first statement: "La procesión del año: / cambios que son repeticiones" [The year's procession: / changes that are repetitions]. By crossing two of the three pairs defined by Oviedo, Paz now combines water and light.[9] What is normally seen as light is now expressed as water ("La madrugada: más que luz, vaho / de claridad cambiada en gotas grávidas" [Dawn: more than light, / a vapor of clarity / changed into gravid drops], a development of a key verse from the previous section, "la luz es agua, el agua tiempo diáfano" (VI,27) [light is water; water, diaphanous time]. Time, expressed in the sixth section as water "donde los ojos lavan sus imágenes" [where eyes wash their images] is here "luz filtrada" [filtered light]. The fig tree, whose leaves had created the isolation of a separate world, is now the bare symbol of this section's theme of permanence and change. The section's conclusion, contrasting light and shadow, emphasizes, in its use of "se derrama" [overflows] as the final verb, the duality of light and water.

The seventh section functions as an interlude in the sense that it does not advance the narrative of the poem, or rather as a bridge between the larger subjects of the fig tree and the first encounter with literature. Yet the fig tree is not put aside once it has been recalled and evaluated, but seen in a different way as time moves forward. In this way the poem grows by accretion, avoids a linear pattern, and develops the concept of revision suggested by the title.

The eighth section is Paz's tribute to the importance of literature in his intellectual formation. More than a recitation of favorite authors (including Garcilaso, Nerval, Dante, Villaurrutia, and Verne), the poet testifies to the power of books to create a reality more structured and meaningful than his observable world, in the same way that the world of the fig tree was more vivid and vital than the patio in which it stood. This section also traces, briefly but unforgettably, the origin of two attitudes that are the foundations of all of Paz's work: the twin mysteries of eroticism and poetic inspiration. The former is deeply involved in his passionate approach to the world. The latter suggests a magical gift (or burden) that forces him constantly to create (or re-create) meaning, and leads him again to the awareness of writing, which has not been explicitly recalled since the beginning of the fifth section. Now he progresses from words to names to images that "acumulan sus gaseosas, / conjeturales confederaciones" [their vaporous conjectural confederations]. In an uncharacteristically musical and onomatopoetic outburst, he uses clouds to suggest the value of literature in his youth:

> Nubes y nubes, fantasmal galope
> de las nubes sobre las crestas
> de mi memoria. Adolescencia,
> país de nubes.
> [VIII,52-55]

> [Clouds and clouds, a phantom gallop
> of clouds over the peaks
> of my memory. Adolescence,
> land of clouds.]

The ninth section is another brief transition, here bridging the subjects of literature and the family house. Framed by

both introductory and concluding statements on the time-
less memory of the plaza in which the house is situated, this
section is a composite of pleasant impressions that appeal to
the senses. Perspective, form, light, and color are the basis of
the vision, but taste and touch are strongly supportive. In the
compact development of twenty-one verses, the poet has
included a still life, an impressionistic miniature that records
his pleasure in remembering the locale of his boyhood. With
the linking of the first verse of the tenth section, he advances
to the interior of his home.

The linking is combined in the first reference to his
awareness of writing after the equally brief reference at the
beginning of the fifth section: "Mis palabras, / al hablar de la
casa, se agrietan" [My words, / speaking of the house, split
apart]. The use of "se agrietan" is striking in its depiction of
internal stress (both in the poet's personality and in his lan-
guage) and the suggestion of forces behind words. Having
touched on the act of writing, Paz develops other subjects,
returning to it again in a fuller development in the twelfth
section. In this way he reminds the reader that he is periodi-
cally aware of the creative act as he writes the poem.

The portrait of the poet's family life in the tenth section
provides interesting material for a psychoanalyst. Unlike the
sun-drenched and idyllic portrait of the plaza that imme-
diately precedes it, the description of the family is dominated
by rancor, loneliness, and disorientation. The definition of all
families in terms of his is bitterly critical:

                    . . . Familias,
          criaderas de alacranes:
          como a los perros dan con la pitanza
          vidrio molido, nos alimentan con sus odios
                              [X,6-9]

                    [. . . . Families,
          breeding-grounds for scorpions:
          as they give ground glass to dogs
          with their pittance, so they nourish us with hates]

This is not to say that the portrait is completely negative. The poet recognizes the value of solitude and communion with nature and the strength he derived from his mother, his aunt, and his grandfather, each of whom is succinctly portrayed. The relationship with his father, whose alcoholism and horrible death under a train are graphically described, is meaningless, and acquires substance only in the poet's dreams. This section stands out not only in the poem, but in all of Paz's work, for its clarity and candor. The clinical objectivity with which he dissects the members of his family, his relationship with them, and his own character could not have been arrived at easily. The fact that in numerous interviews and biographical studies Paz's family did not emerge with the fullness given them here is understandable. What is particularly dramatic is the need, created by the poem's subject, to put aside the traditional privacy of Hispanic family life. That Paz could do so successfully, against his previous unwillingness to develop such personal subjects, is a commentary on the extent of his commitment to poetry.

In an expressive juxtaposition of verbs at the conclusion of this section, the poet's objectivity toward himself underscores the timeless world of memory: "Fui (soy) yerba, maleza / entre escombros anónimos" [I was (I am) grass, / weeds in anonymous trash]. In thus merging past and present, particularly against the background of the crumbling house of the previous verse, the poet makes an equivalence that is essentially a paradox. The past recalled is indeed the present. Time is as meaningless as its resolution, earlier in this section, in "simulacros de reflejos" [simulacra of reflections], a brilliant metaphor suggesting that multiple perceptions of time conceal its ultimate reality.

Oviedo accurately interprets this section's subject as the Tantric road to knowledge of oneself and of the world: "Entre otras cosas, el pensamiento tántrico nos dice que sólo conocemos a través de la experiencia . . . . La verdadera realidad es esa fusión de los dobles (o mitades: macho y hembra), imantación que se repite en todas las escalas como un principio universal"[10] [Among other things, Tantric thought tells

us that we only know through experience . . . . True reality is
that fusion of doubles (or halves: male and female), an attrac-
tion that is repeated in all scales as a universal principle].
Paz's goal here, as in *Piedra de sol* and other poems, is to reach
the center of life in which time and dualities do not exist:
"Esto confirma oportunamente lo que ya señalé antes: por
más personal que parezca el poema, ese yo que habla y medita
y goza no es una voz individual aislada del mundo, sino
seguramente la *voz del mundo*, la poesía hecha por todos que
quería Lautréamont"[11] [This confirms opportunely what I
indicated before: however personal the poem may seem, that
"I" that speaks and meditates and enjoys is not an individual
voice isolated from the world, but surely the *voice of the
world*, the poetry composed by everybody that Lautréamont
wanted].

There is another, perhaps less important but nonetheless
pertinent, interpretation of the eleventh section that Oviedo
does not cite, its "narrative" as autoeroticism. The poet
declares that his body, in different forms, spoke to him (verse
13). The references to the succubus and the feminine odor of
plants (verses 17-18) and the ecstasy of lines 29-32 clearly
suggest a solitary sexual climax, whose aftermath is a percep-
tion that time has been broken and that he is two persons in
one. This ambiguity of interpretation is designed, as Paz has
often indicated in his criticism, not to force the reader to
choose between alternatives, even though they seem mutu-
ally exclusive, but to help him join divergent interpretations
in the perception of life's underlying unity.

The concern with writing and language returns as the
major subject of the twelfth section, introduced by a triangle
of successive unrealities: time, flesh, and word. Paz here
approaches language through the emptiness of death, a noth-
ingness without which creation would not have meaning:
"La muerte es madre de las formas" (XII,10) [Death is the
mother of forms]. Dwelling on the sound of the word
"muerte" makes the poet feel its meaning briefly. His con-
centration on the page he has just written, and his observa-
tion that words, like amphibians, can change from one

element to another, endow words with an independent existence. Their obscure origin is the unknown side of life. Most important for the development of the theme of poetry is the conclusion, which suggests that the meaning of words may be impossible to define.

The consciousness of language and writing links the twelfth and thirteenth sections: "Salto de un cuento a otro / por un puente colgante de once sílabas" [I leap from one story to another on a / suspension bridge of eleven syllables]. The subject of language changes abruptly, however, in favor of reflections on the nature of air.[12] Significantly, its description takes on the characteristics of the other three elements, with water predominating. The air "amanece rocío" [wakes up as dew], it is the "nadador en la mar brava del fuego" [swimmer in the rough seas of fire], an "invisible surtidor de ayes" [invisible fountain of laments], and can lift two oceans with a hand.

Almost in the middle of this section, the implication of the poet's awareness of himself in the midst of creative activity returns with a question: "¿Y para qué digo todo esto?" [And why do I say all this?]. The break, however, is not as abrupt as it might seem, for the rest of this section discusses two similar creatures of the air, butterflies and moths, the first at noon and the latter, the "cabeza de muerto" and "mensajera de las ánimas," at night. The two halves of this section, which seem at first reading to be unrelated, are joined by the Psyche reference in the last verse, particularly by the name's Greek origin as the breath of life.

Although the fourteenth section is, except for the conclusion, the briefest in the poem, it advances both the review of the poet's life and his thoughts about writing:

¿Hay mensajeros? Sí,
cuerpo tatuado de señales
es el espacio, el aire es invisible
tejido de llamadas y respuestas.
Animales y cosas se hacen lenguas,
a través de nosotros habla consigo mismo

el universo. Somos un fragmento
—pero cabal en su inacabamiento—
de su discurso. Solipsismo
coherente y vacío:
desde el principio del principio
¿qué dice? Dice que nos dice.
Se lo dice a sí mismo. *Oh madness of discourse,*
that cause sets up with and against itself!

                              [Are there messengers? Yes,
space is a body tattooed with signs, the air
an invisible web of calls and answers.
Animals and things make languages,
through us the universe talks with itself.
We are a fragment—
accomplished in our unaccomplishment—
of its discourse. A coherent
and empty solipsism:
since the beginning of the beginning
what does it say? It says that it says us.
It says it to itself. *Oh madness of discourse*
that cause sets up with and against itself!

As in so many of the transitions that we have noted, there
is a linking between the thirteenth and fourteenth sections
by means of the opening verse: "¿Hay mensajeros? Sí" con-
tinues the previous statement of the moth as "mensajero de
las ánimas." A more important continuity is the elaboration
of the previous section's first subject, air, as a web of calls and
answers. If animals and things become tongues with which
the universe speaks to itself, then the poet's review of his
memories is a part of the same process. Whatever order he
gives it, whatever conclusions he draws, are therefore imper-
sonal. Although there may be an order of which he is a part,
man will not be able to understand it.

    This section is also unique in making a statement that is
equally important to the narrative of memory and the nar-
rative of writing. The universe reduces itself to a solipsism.
Paz has gone beyond the meaning implied in his commentary

on words at the end of the twelfth section, in which "decir" differs from "hablar" by conveying a message. Here the message is defined in terms of itself; who is speaking and what is being said are mysteries beyond the poet's comprehension. There is another innovation in this section that will prevail for the remainder of the poem, the joining of the two major themes. Although writing and memory have been closely related, they have been treated separately until now. They have been interwoven, rather than fused, in a braid that began with the poem. They have been two entities, whose natures the reader compares and contrasts in the first thirteen sections. In fact, memory serves as the basis for one reading of the title, the past seen clearly, and writing for another, the revision of thought that gives meaning to expression. Now the solipsism described here applies equally to both, so that writing becomes a part of memory and vice versa, and both become a part of the universe's dialogue with itself. They will continue merged for the rest of the poem.

The fifteenth section begins with the probing of the word "muerte," first stated in the twelfth section. The meaning of the fourth verse here ("Y yo en la muerte descubrí el lenguaje" [And in death I discovered language] involves the consideration of language against a background of nothingness. It is, at the same time, what men use to communicate with each other, and their communications form history. The poet sees linear time, the tunnels and galleries of history, as the sentence and punishment of mankind, from which death may not be the only exit: "El escape, quizás, es hacia dentro" (XV,29) [The way out, perhaps, is toward within].

In this section Paz returns to an ideal world, fully developed in *Ladera este* but enumerated long before in *Piedra de sol* and some of the poems of *Libertad bajo palabra*, in which time and pronouns are abolished: "ni *yo soy* ni *yo más* sino más ser sin yo" (XV,32) [not *I am* nor *I even more so* but more being without I]. If there is one pronoun whose dissolution he desires more intensely than the others, it is the first person singular. The center of time can be described only by paradoxes: fixed movement, or a circle counteracted by its revolutions. As the poem approaches its conclusion and the final definition of the poet's experiences, language (and writing, the record of the creative act) serves as the metaphor for all meaning.

The sixteenth section represents another quiet and reflective moment before a further advance in the quest, now with dominant imagery of fire and light. (Two references in verses 15 and 28 to other elements, however, provide contrasts that accentuate the dominant imagery: "la respiración del viento" [the breathing of the wind] and "llama en el tallo de agua" [flame on the water-stalk].) The subjects represent a kaleidoscopic, peaceful selection of items from a landscape: noon, autumn, the sun on the poet's writing, and a series of philosophical reflections based on the latter. The general movement in this section clearly follows a progression from concreteness to abstraction, but the final reference to "un tercer estado" leads to a more specific enumeration of the object of the quest than Paz has provided until now.

This section also represents a continuation of the merging of the poem's two themes noted in the fourteenth section. Beginning with the observation of sunlight falling on his words ("El sol en mi escritura bebe sombra" [The sun, in my writing, drinks the shadows], the poet sees a remembered grove, inhabited by the spirit of time:

> El dios sin cuerpo, el dios sin nombre
> que llamamos con nombres
> vacíos—con los nombres del vacío—,
> el dios del tiempo, el dios que es tiempo,
> pasa entre los ramajes
> que escribo.
>   [XVI, 16-21]
>
> [The bodiless god, the nameless god
> whom we call by empty names—
> by the names of the emptiness—
> the god of time, the god that is time,
> passes through the branches
> that I write.]

External reality thus mingles with the objective of his creative activity, so that the imaginative terms he uses become the thing he is attempting to describe:

> Llama en el tallo de agua
> de las palabras que la dicen,
> la flor es otro sol.
>   [XVI, 28-30]
>
> [Flame on the water-stalk
> of the words that say it,
> the flower is another sun.]

This fusion adumbrates the conclusion of the poem (section XIX), in which the poet follows the same process, applying it to himself. Its importance in this section is to identify the consequences to the poet of the merging of opposites, which provides the overwhelming impression of transcendence at the section's conclusion, constructed in progressively longer verses of seven, nine, eleven, and fourteen syllables to emphasize the final verse of seven syllables:

> La quietud en sí misma
> se disuelve. Transcurre el tiempo
> sin transcurrir. Pasa y se queda. Acaso,
> aunque todos pasamos, ni pasa ni se queda:
> hay un tercer estado.
>   [XVI, 31-35]
>
> [Tranquility dissolves in itself. Time
> elapses without elapse. It passes and stays. Perhaps
> although we all pass, it neither passes nor stays:
> there is a third state.]

The reconciliation of opposites is the subject of the seventeenth section, which begins with words that are almost identical to the conclusion of the sixteenth, but which in their changed order emphasize "tercer" rather than "estado." This state goes beyond bliss to fulfillment, beyond awareness to knowledge, and beyond knowledge to something greater.

Oviedo attaches unusual importance to the verse "no la presencia: su presentimiento" [not the presence: its presentiment]:

> En él está encerrada una idea fundamental en la poética de Paz: el lenguaje como presentimiento de una divinidad (un poco después dirá francamente de ella: «Es Dios», v. 578) o presencia inalcanzable fuera de la experiencia que llamamos poema. La poesía es una tensión perpetua que apunta hacia ese blanco del que sólo tenemos fulguraciones, ráfagas; a través de ellas la realidad revela su verdadera faz—la faz que niegan las evidencias.[13]

> [In it is enclosed an idea fundamental to the poetics of Paz: language as presentiment of a divinity (a little later he will say frankly of it: "It is God," v. 578) or presence that is unattainable outside of the experience that we call poem. Poetry is a perpetual tension that aims at that target of which we have only flashes, gusts; through them reality reveals its real face—the face denied by evidence.]

It is ironic that the poet must use language to describe meaning beyond it. The repetition of "nombres," "confluencias del lenguaje," the description of "nada" as a "palabra de dos filos, palabra entre dos huecos" [double-edged word, word between two hollows], and its variant "entre los blancos del discurso" [in the pauses of speech] identify language as the external form of the meaning that the poet has been seeking from the outset of the poem. Like other attempts to define an ultimate reality, particularly the "estado tercero," the conclusion of this section can be expressed only in terms of a paradox: "aparecía en cada forma / de desvanecimiento" [It appeared in every form / of vanishing].

The predictable link to the eighteenth section is the concept of divinity for which the poet attempts to find a unique name. Here, at the very end of his quest, the search for meaning is expressed completely in terms of the writer's struggle with expression. As he had done more than twenty-seven years before in "Las palabras," Paz vents his distaste for the shabby and broken words that he must choose from. After enormous time and effort, the result of his creativity is remarkably fragile:

> Espiral de los ecos, el poema
> es aire que se esculpe y se disipa,
> fugaz alegoría de los nombres
> verdaderos.
>   [XVIII,24-27]

> [Spiral of echoes, the poem
> is air that sculpts itself and dissolves,
> a fleeting allegory of true names.]

It is, then, only an impermanent approximation of meaning. The dominant impression of poetry, even though the poet says that it happens only "a veces," is movement or meaning that constantly flows and rearranges itself. The implication is that it is in the movement, not any particular arrangement, that poetry exists.

Significantly, the search for expression has merged so with memory's search for meaning that the latter no longer exists. The poem begins with the quest for meaning, in which the concern for expression is only a personal footnote. As the poet focuses on his objective and the means of defining it, he finds himself concentrating more on his efforts as the key to that objective. Finally, he discovers that it is only the effort, the poetic process more than the poem, that provides meaning. There is no perceptible structure in a universe that speaks only to itself; there is no divinity; and there is no author of creation other than the poet, who can only study the symbols that he has set down for a clue to the meaning of life. Oviedo selects verses 18 and 19 for special attention ("Alcé con las palabras y sus sombras / una casa ambulante de reflejos" [I built with words and their shadows / a movable house of reflections]:

Estas dos líneas están hinchadas de significación y se
proyectan hacia muchos lados: si las palabras son el ser,
sus *sombras* son la muerte (los contrarios que com-
baten) y eso se vincula con la noción de casa (casa de los
muertos, casa en la que vivió): casa en movimiento, sin
embargo (nueva contradicción) que proyecta reflejos, es,
pues, la totalidad misma porque incluye a su contrario
en la fugacidad de su abrazo sensual.[14]

[These two lines are overflowing with significance and
project themselves in many directions: if words are
being, their *shadows* are death (opposites in conflict)
and that is related to the notion of house (house of the
dead, house in which he lived): house in movement,
nevertheless (new contradiction) that projects reflec-
tions is, then, totality itself because it includes its op-
posite in the fleetingness of its sensual embrace.]

The final brief section is an epilogue to the conclusion of
the poem in the eighteenth section. Its achievement is to
close the circle with the poem's initiation: "Estoy en donde
estuve:" [I am where I was:]. The same inner steps that began
the poem are heard, with a notable difference. They are now
with eyes (reason and conscious effort) rather than with the
soul (feeling and unconscious awareness). In contrast to the
introduction's unwillingness to accept the steps, we have
now the poet's firm definition not only that those steps are
his, but also that they represent all that he is. In contrast to
his vanishing words and the ruins of speech at the beginning,
the epilogue affirms that he hears the voices that he thinks,
which by being heard, create him. The final verse, "Soy la
sombra que arrojan mis palabras," states that the poet him-
self is less substantial than his creation. Thus poetry is a
necessity for existence.

The circularity of *Pasado en claro* has the same effect
noted in *Piedra de sol.* Even if the ending were identical to the
beginning, as it is not in *Pasado en claro,* the meaning cannot
be the same because the poem itself has intervened. The
readers have been changed, although in intangible and di-

verse ways, by their reading. That effect is intensified in *Pasado en claro* by the subtle but symbolic alterations of the introductory material described above.

Pasado en claro differs from other works in making an additional demand on the reader. It takes form in the poet's emphasis on writing, language, and the poetic process. As we have seen, this is present in Paz's work from the first major work in his poetic career, the first edition of *Libertad bajo palabra* in 1949. Until the composition of *Pasado en claro*, language and writing were a subsidiary theme of major works or the major theme of a few individual poems, and did not assume, as they do here, the dimension of a philosophy. The latest (we certainly cannot assume final) form of this theme is most fully understood in the context of its earlier development, which adds breadth and interest to the comprehension of the poem. The demand on the reader, therefore, is to read *Pasado en claro* in the context of Paz's earlier poetry.

A further demand of *Pasado en claro* involves the reader's participation in the poetic process. The circularity of *Piedra de sol* requires a rereading of the poem with a new perspective of time. In the case of *Blanco*, the emphasis is on the multiplicity and the relationships of several themes. *Ladera este* employs a series of denials and affirmations, of paradoxes and polarities, to reach a resolution of opposites. All three techniques, essentially, broaden the reader's understanding of the poems and enlarge his vision of reality. They bring him to the edge of the creative process, but do not compel his collaboration in the writing of the poem.

In *Pasado en claro* the invitation to participate in the poem is stronger than in its predecessors. Although the poet's quest is personal—as we have seen, no other poem by Paz is more so—the reader's identification with the poet requires him to initiate his own journey of exploration: "Así, la vida personal es una apertura a la memoria de todos los hombres; memoria total. Lenguaje total"[15] [Thus personal life is an opening to the memory of all men; total memory. Total language]. The vagueness of the poem's first two sections and of the final one particularly compel the reader to ask the poem's questions of his own experience. Since the poet's objective is "ni *yo soy* ni

yo más sino más ser sin yo," the first person singular of the
final verse becomes a collective plural: we are all the shadows
cast by our words. In this sense Paz's attempt to define reality
through memory is significant not for its autobiographical
details, but for its definition of a process in which the reader
participates, perhaps not so much during his reading of the
poem as during his subsequent reflection on it. The most
important consequence, therefore, is not the poem's con-
clusion, but the one that the reader eventually creates.

Perhaps the most useful interpretation of *Pasado en claro*
comes indirectly from the poet himself. In his lucid analysis
of one of the most hermetic artists of Surrealism, Marcel
Duchamp, Paz contrasts his work with that of Picasso. If the
latter is the painter of time and images, Duchamp presents
movement and meditation on the image (just as, we may add,
Pasado en claro presents a poem on poetry). Where Picasso
affirms through exuberance of quantity and tone, Duchamp
negates through intense irony and a very limited artistic
production that led to withdrawal from the "artistic" world,
the poet's equivalent of silence.[16]

Paz's affinity with Duchamp reveals itself through the
latter's fascination with language, which was for this modern
Renaissance man's definition of reality as significant as
mathematics, chess, philosophy, or humor. In his "Green
Box," for example, he suggested the search for "prime
words," divisible only by themselves and by unity.[17] Even
more important for the comprehension of *Pasado en claro* is
Paz's emphasis on Duchamp's negation of technique: the
ready-mades not only criticize taste but also attack the con-
cept of the work of art. The artist is not a craftsman but a
creator of acts. We can apply Paz's judgment of Duchamp to
much of the poet's own work in his unwillingness to dissoci-
ate form and content: "La forma proyecta sentido, es un
aparato de significar"[19] [Form projects sense, it is a signifying
machine].

The most significant commentary on the similarity be-
tween Paz and Duchamp is the poet's reference to Mallarmé's
poem, "Un Coup de dés." In quoting himself, which, proba-

bly through selectivity as much as modesty, he rarely does,
Paz radically redefines both the objective and the nature of
poetry. Mallarmé's work is a critical poem

> que contiene su propia negación y que hace de esa nega-
> ción el punto de partida del canto, a igual distancia de
> afirmación y negación . . . . Mallarmé enfrenta dos
> posibilidades en apariencia excluyentes (el acto y su
> omisión, el azar y el absoluto) y, sin suprimirlas, las
> resuelve en una afirmación condicional—una afirma-
> ción que sin cesar se niega y así se afirma pues se
> alimenta de su propia negación.[19]

> [that contains its own negation and that makes of that
> negation the point of departure of the song, equidistant
> from affirmation and negation . . . . Mallarmé faces
> two possibilities apparently exclusive (the act and its
> omission, chance and the absolute), and without sup-
> pressing them, resolves them in a conditional affirma-
> tion—an affirmation that ceaselessly denies itself and
> thus affirms itself since it feeds on its own negation.]

The effect of this dialectic between affirmation and nega-
tion—as applicable to Paz as to Mallarmé and Duchamp—is
to change the reader or spectator into a collaborator. The
possibility of multiple interpretation, which is very different
from ambiguity, leaves the creation of the final word to the
reader:

> Imagen que refleja a la imagen de aquel que la con-
> templa, jamás podremos verla sin vernos a nosotros
> mismos . . . . Es verdad que el espectador crea una obra
> distinta a la imaginada por el artista pero entre una y
> otra obra, entre lo que el artista *quiso* hacer y lo que el
> espectador *cree* ver, hay una *realidad:* la obra.[20]

> [Image that reflects the image of the one who con-
> templates it, we shall never be able to see it without
> seeing ourselves . . . . It is true that the spectator cre-

ates a work different from the one imagined by the
artist, but between one work and the other, between
what the artist *tried* to do and what the spectator *thinks*
that he sees, there is a *reality*: the work.]

Pasado en claro, accordingly, is not a poem in the conven-
tional sense but an "aparato de significar."

7 *Vuelta*
Toward Silence

Para callar es necesario haberse arriesgado a decir.

[In order to be silent, it is necessary to have risked saying
   something.]

                 —Paz, *Poesía en movimiento*

Like all poetry, *Vuelta* represents man's attempt
to define the world and his place in it; like Paz's other works,
this definition rests on the poet's quest for identity that is at
the same time common to all men. Completely apart from
the meaning that this work conveys to the reader unac-
quainted with the poet's other works is the comprehension of
Vuelta as the result of all Paz's poetry after *Ladera este*. The
opportunity to gain the fullest meaning of the poems through
seeing them in the context of the poet's development is the
latest (but almost certainly not the last) demand that this
poet makes on his readers.

    That demand is articulated most clearly in the book's first
section, "Configuraciones," whose eight poems are all on the
themes of language, poetry, and the art of reading the poem.
Although the relationship among these is not always stated
by the poet, it is essential to the full comprehension of each of
these poems. In fact, the reader is expected to establish the
relationship himself if he follows the cues.

    "A vista de pájaro" ["Bird's-eye View"], the brief introduc-
tory poem, uses the flight of a bird as a subject that seems far
removed from the introspective concern of the writer exam-
ining his own work:

             Furiosamente
                    gira
          sobre un reflejo
              cae

en línea recta
            afilada
blancura
            asciende
ya sangriento el pico
sal dispersa
            apenas línea
al caer
      recta
tu mirada
            sobre esta página
disuelta

[Furiously
            wheels
on a reflection
            falls
in a straight line
                  sharpened
whiteness
            ascends
its beak already bloodied
salt scattered
                  barely a line
as it falls
            straight
your glance
            on this page
dissolved]

The strength of the first exclamatory verses ("Furiosamen-
te / gira"), the strong action verbs that follow ("cae", "as-
ciende"), the straight line that marks the bird's fall on his
unidentified prey, and the implied narrative of "ya sangriento
el pico" constitute a re-created reality. The reader's first reac-
tion is that he is witnessing a scene of nature which the poet
is photographing through his words. In that sense the poem is
moving toward the object, which is the action of the bird.
Through the masterful transition of verses 11-13, which in-

troduce without punctuation the final three verses, the bird's
flight becomes the reader's glance on the printed page. It is
only at the end of the poem that we realize that not only has
the bird not been named, but that no subject has been given
for the verbs noted above. If the reader logically assumes that
the subject is the bird of the title, he reacts to the suggestion
of the metaphor that becomes the center of the poem's mean-
ing.

The strength of the metaphor is intensified by the boldness
of withholding punctuation even at the end of the poem,
causing, like the circular lines of *Piedra de sol* that are both
introduction and conclusion, a rereading of the poem. The
words "tu mirada / sobre esta página / disuelta" in the final
and climactic position not only invite but require further
reading, thought, and feeling. The "bird," then, becomes the
reader's comprehension, whose prey is the poem and whose
accuracy is stressed by the repetition of the straight line that
it pursues. There is, nonetheless, a difference in the restate-
ment: "cae / en línea recta" becomes, after the central divid-
ing line of the poem's construction ("ya sangriento el pico"),
"apenas línea / al caer / recta." In the restatement, the bird-
glance is seen as the abandonment of its form as it dissolves
on the page. The reader concludes that his comprehension
has shaped his reading. He has, in some mysterious way,
altered the form of the poem.

A similar theme and construction shape two other poems
of this group, "Por la calle de Galeana" ["Along Galeana
Street"] and "La arboleda" ["The Grove"]. The former not
only avoids punctuation completely, but also uses lower-case
letters to begin sentences (as in verses 6, 8, 13) so that the
joining of disparate ideas suggests a stream of consciousness:

> Golpean martillos allá arriba
>   voces pulverizadas
> Desde la punta de la tarde bajan
>   verticalmente los albañiles
>
> Estamos entre azul y buenas noches
>   aquí comienzan los baldíos

Un charco anémico de pronto llamea
    la sombra de un colibrí lo incendia
Al llegar a las primeras casas
    el verano se oxida
Alguien ha cerrado la puerta alguien
    habla con su sombra
Pardea ya no hay nadie en la calle
    ni siquiera este perro
    asustado de andar solo por ella
    Da miedo cerrar los ojos

[Hammers pound there above
    pulverized voices
From the top of the afternoon
    the builders come straight down
We're between blue and good evening
    here begin vacant lots
A pale puddle suddenly blazes
    the shade of the hummingbird ignites it
Reaching the first houses
    the summer oxidizes
Someone has closed the door   someone
    speaks with his shadow
It darkens   There's no one in the street now
    not even this dog
scared to walk through it alone
    One's afraid to close one's eyes]

Like "A vista de pájaro," the title's definition of the subject
identifies a fragment of reality—in this case a street scene—
that the poem describes in considerable detail. The final
verse, contrasting strongly in tone with the tranquil descrip-
tion of minutia of the first fifteen verses, raises a profound
question about the meaning of that reality and in doing so
opens a new vista that calls for a rereading of the poem.
    The answer is found more in the "factual" description of
the street scene than in the mystery of the concluding state-

ment. Each phenomenon of the street scene is the result of a perception that is touched by magic, and in each what is ordinary reality is subordinated to the power of a sensory or esthetic impression. The effect of the hammers is to pulverize the voices of the men wielding them, the reflection of the hummingbird ignites the pond, and the summer light becomes rusty as it strikes the houses. The logical action of closing a door not only is a part of the scene's magical atmosphere, but is linked with the "illogical" action of someone's dialogue with his shadow. The climax of this transformation of reality into something that is at the same time more intangible and more real is the denial in the last stanza of the evidence of one's senses: even the dog, which is so visible that one can see that he too is frightened by the solitude, does not exist.

In this way the reader is prepared for the conflict of realities suggested by the final verse. If the description of the street scene is more complete, more tangible, and more meaningful than the scene itself, then reality resides not in the object but in the poet's impressions. Yet since he recognizes the difficulty of conveying those impressions and of assuming that they will be the same for the reader, he cannot accept them as final. The result is a metaphysical problem: if a person closes his eyes, he may not be able to reenter the world he has left. Although not as explicitly as in "A vista de pájaro," the reader is invited to reread the poem in the perspective of the revelation fully expressed only in the final verse, and to create his own solution to this problem of perception.

In "La arboleda" Paz employs the same technique of transforming reality through the implications of the final verse. Although much longer and supported by conventional punctuation, the description here also probes appearances. The paradoxical nature of the grove is emphasized in the parallelism of the first four verses. Within it every element of description contributes to the miraculous reconstruction of the natural scene. Just as the visible but nonexistent dog of "Por la calle de Galeana" foreshadows the climax, so here the

patio and its contents isolate themselves in the growing
darkness, preparing the reader for the deeper transformation
of the final verse. As the objects of the patio become only
"sacos de sombra" [nothing but shadows], and space closes in
on itself, their reality is felt without words. Language, then,
becomes unnecessary if the reader has perceived the poem's
objective. The unwritten conclusion is supplied by the read-
er.[1]

The paradox that introduces "Palabras en forma de
tolvanera" ["Words in the Form of a Dust Cloud"] clearly
defines the poem's subject not as an element of external
reality, as in the three poems just examined, but as an internal
landscape that finds expression in the poem that is being
written. Again, a paradox—the window that opens on no-
where but that also opens on the poet's personal landscape—
introduces the poem. In contrast to the three previous com-
positions, in which the poem was referred to explicitly only
in the conclusion, if at all, the act of writing ("Caben / en esta
hoja" [They fit / on this sheet])is an integral part of the
poem's early development. The subject of the first of the
poem's two stanzas is the turbulence of formless impressions
that might be contained on paper if their movement could be
halted. After the poem describes the turning of the page that
marks the end of the stanza, the "instantáneas li-
vianas / torres de polvo giratorio" [floating snapshots / tow-
ers of whirling dust] become "Torbellinos de ecos"
[Whirlwinds of echoes]. Although they are the raw material
from which the poem might be fashioned, they move into
other open spaces, suggesting a dimension even more distant
from the poet. The only clue to their meaning is that it is
different from the words, which are, paradoxically, always
different and always the same. Somewhere between the op-
posites—or joining them—is the poem.

The conclusion, based again on the openness of unpunctu-
ated form, separates the poet and the reader from the poem:
"Palabras del poema / no las decimos nunca / El poema nos
dice" [We never say / the words of the poem / The poem says
us]. The object pronoun "nos," which now includes the read-

er, recalls the "yo" of the first verse, which can now be read with an additional interpretation. What seemed like a completely voluntary and conscious act, the opening of the window, has been in fact also unconscious, for it was dictated by the obscure forces that generate language and poetry. To pursue them, to define them, and to confine them in words on paper is the poet's impossible and unavoidable mission. "El fuego de cada día" ["The Everyday Fire"], a double allusion to dawn and to poetry, is the poet's praise of man's greatest gift. The poem's construction rests on the simile that introduces the theme: as air functions in geology and the formation of the universe, so does man's language form reality against the void. The vitality of language, its "electricity," is expressed by "quemante" [burning] and "incandescencias" [incandescences], both of which are adumbrated by the title. In a dramatic shift of metaphors after the first verse of the second stanza, Paz seems to seek a better form for his definition: "También son plantas: " [And they are plants:]. The metaphor of syllables as plants, different as it is from the introductory one of air, shares the attribute of a vital energy. These plants have the ability to change their surroundings through synesthesia as their roots fracture silence and their branches construct structures of sound. The fire of the title reappears in "árboles incandescentes" [incandescent trees] and "vegetaciones de relámpagos" [foliage of lightning].

The poem's conclusion reiterates the generative force of poetry with a closing simile that both parallels and completes the introductory one:

> sobre la hoja de papel
> el poema se hace
>   como el día
> sobre la palama del espacio.

> [on a leaf of paper
> the poem constructs itself
>   like day
> on the palm of space.]

Poetry, then, is a daily miracle, a universal force, and a basic—
perhaps unique—source of life, and this poem is a hymn in its
praise. The implication, which is frequent in French and
Hispanic Surrealist poets, is that the reader should recognize
poetry's integrating role as the modern substitute for philoso-
phy and religion.

"Paisaje inmemorial" ("Immemorial Landscape") is ex-
ceptional in imagery, diction, and musicality in Paz's work,
recalling the poetry in vogue some fifty years before its com-
position. Yet its theme, revealed in the eight concluding
verses, is unmistakably related to Paz's other poems. Perhaps
it is this combination of atypical form with a typical theme
that makes it such a captivating composition, as if the poet
wished to demonstrate that profundity and eloquence are not
limited to a single tonality.

"Paisaje inmemorial" describes a snow scene in three
stanzas, of which two, the first and third, of approximately
equal length, portray the falling snowflakes. The suspense of
the adjectives graphically intensifies the delicate balance of
the snow's descent:

cae
oblicua
ya azul
sobre la otra nieve

[it falls
aslant
now blue
on the other snow]

Between the quiet rhythms and delicate effects of these two
stanzas is the action of the second stanza, whose subject is
the movement of automobiles. Here all the verbs and their
effects suggest strong, occasionally violent, activity. The con-
trast between tranquility and action could not be more em-
phatic.

In the final stanza, like a musical composition returning to
its original theme, the poem returns to the quiet treatment of

falling snow, now with a symbolic objective. The repetition in sequence of three sentences beginning "Un día" constitutes a prophecy. Furthermore, each of the five verbs of this stanza employs the future tense. The reader, therefore, is prepared for the future snow to be "La misma de ahora" [The same as tonight] but not to learn that both are "la nieve de hace un millón de años" [the million year old snow]. Paz's snow scene achieves what he has defined so often in his essays as the abolition of linear time. Although he has not needed to refer to the act of writing here, he has created the timeless experience to which poetry aspires. If we can borrow terminology associated with the criticism of fiction, he shows rather than tells.

Seen in isolation, "Paisaje inmemorial" is an unusually graceful and profound commentary on a wintry experience that seems to have nothing in common with the other poems in this group, whose theme is language and poetry. Yet one should not overlook the arrangement of compositions in a volume, which is one of the conventional methods for the author to indicate how the poem might be read. By including it with seven poems whose subject is the reading of the poem, Paz adds a dimension to the interpretation of "Paisaje inmemorial." More than a commentary on a personal experience, it is a demonstration of the permanence and universality of the recording of that experience. The poem, like the snow, fuses past, present, and future time, and in its essence remains unchanging in its ability to transform the world.

"Trowbridge St." (whose title, one assumes, was the poet's address while teaching at Harvard) is a tightly constructed poem in six sections, occupying the major place in this part of the book before the three very brief graphic poems of "Anotaciones / Rotaciones." Indicating a symmetry that is infrequent in Paz's work, five of the six numbered sections are of equal length—ten verses in each. Only the third section, on the theme of air, exceeds that number with eighteen verses, which can be reduced to twelve if one subtracts the six verses that are simply repetitions of "El aire." Rather than the development of a single theme, the sections represent six separate themes which the reader may fit together into a meaningful whole. The first section is the empty and cold background against which the action of the other sections takes place. With the exception of the central verses ("Todavía no hay nieve / hay viento viento" [Still no snow / but wind wind], there is no action; except for the final verse, which is a transition to the monologue of the second section, there is no sound. The dominant elements of the wintry days are the sun and the cold, whose opposition is expressed in the oxymora of verses 2 and 7-8. The theme, then, is an abstraction of silence and static objects, whose tension is implied. The poet chooses a little red tree as the focal point of his thoughts.

In the second section, the poet views himself with the same objectivity that he uses for the winter scene of the first section. He stands, symbolically, in an abandoned room of language, addressing a "tú" that the reader assumes, only from the evidence of many other poems, is his beloved. Very unusual here is the double focus of the poet's vision, in which he gives the reader a choice of two realities that may not be different:

> Estoy en un cuarto abandonado del lenguaje
> Tú estás en otro cuarto idéntico
> O los dos estamos
> en una calle que tu mirada ha despoblado
> [Poemas, 592]

> [I am in a room abandoned by language
> You are in another identical room
> Or we both are
> on a street your glance has depopulated]

What is common to both symbolic scenes is the couple alone, incommunicative, and seen in a void. The fluidity of the vison and its lack of completeness is repeated at the end of the section by the paradoxical dilemma of the poet being stranded in the middle of an unwritten line. The implication of this paradox is the conflict of two realities: the actual experience and one that he is struggling to depict.

The third section's subject is air, as water will be that of the fourth. Seen first as an independent agent that causes the opening and closing of doors and wanders through the house alone speaking to the inhabitants, it later changes its form as it merges with the poet's identity. It invades the poet's mind, devoid of other subjects, and affects the meaning of the poem itself ("El aire / con dedos de aire disipa lo que digo" [Air / with air-fingers scatters everything I say]. At the end of this section, the poet has become air that is ignored by his beloved, yet he lacks the strength to close the doors that were moved by air at the section's beginning.

The fourth section is introduced by the fluidity of three equivalent yet differentiated images based on the repeated pattern of "tiene la forma de." The hour is a pause which is the beloved's form, which is a fountain, not of water but of time. The three fragments of the poet balanced on top of the stream are the past, present, and future of "Paisaje inmemorial," personalized by the first person but depersonalized by the use of the article, as if they were objects: "el fui el soy el no soy todavía" [what I was am still am not]. This process of depersonalization is extended in the following lines, so that all three aspects of the poet's existence—the present of verse 8, the past of verse 9, and the future of 10—dwindle to insignificance.

The fifth section marks the transformation of the beloved, continuing the metamorphoses of the fourth section: "Ahora tienes la forma de un puente" [Now you have a bridge-shape]. Using a duplication of personae, so that the couple see themselves passing under the bridge, Paz merges subject and object in a confusion of identity. This imagery, related to the use of the mirror, is a constant device in his poetry beginning with some of the earliest poems of *Libertad bajo palabra*.[2] The reversal of an image is suggested in the position of the sun, whose roots grow upward and whose branches (the sunset) are a bonfire. The hermetic final verse of this section ("El día es habitable" [the day is habitable]) might mean that the heat of the fire makes the cold day comfortable or that the natural setting has become as tangible as their room.

The final section clearly returns to the setting, imagery,

and tone of the first. In fact, the arrangement of its elements constitutes a precise parallel: the glassy air recalls the cold sun; the silence in which echoes are multiplied recalls the deserted streets; the possibility of snow is identical in both, as is the little red tree in the ninth verse of both sections. Their final verses are identical in meaning, but with a change of emphasis. The conclusion of the first section, "Hablo con él al hablar contigo" [Talking to it I talk to you] becomes in the final verse of the poem "Al hablar con él hablo contigo." The reader feels that since the poem has traversed a full circle, he has returned to the point of origin. Nothing has changed, but the memory of the poem suggests that both the reader and the poet have returned from a journey.

In the same way, the final verses of the four other stanzas recall major recurrent themes in Paz's work. The conclusion of the second stanza continues the central idea of *Pasado en claro.* The final verse of the third (which is a recasting of the conclusion of "La arboleda") is a commentary on the firmness of a reality that is not final. The same can be said for the fifth stanza. The fourth stanza continues the theme of love that is so fully developed in Paz's early poetry.

The three little graphic poems of "Anotaciones / Rotaciones" indicate Paz's continuing interest in the flexibility of poetry so that it can be read not only in different ways, but, more important, so that the reader can feel the simultaneity of multiple meanings. Some contemporary critics have dismissed these experiments, particularly *Topoemas* and *Discos visuales,* as game poems, minor works that display more of a ludic spirit than the mainstream of Paz's achievements. Certainly the casual reader is likely to feel their lack of profundity in comparison with some of the major poems examined here. Seen in the context of the demands that Paz's poems as a whole place upon the reader, however, they reveal, perhaps better than the longer poems, the extent to which the poet seeks openness of form.

"Dos en uno" is a brilliant example of the transformation that a graphic arrangement can make in what would have been a pleasant but ordinary *haiku:*

Baja
desnuda

la luna   la mujer
por el pozo   por mis ojos

[Comes down
nude

the moon   the woman
through the well   through my eyes]

By omitting punctuation and arranging the three couplets in triangular form, Paz emphasizes several elements—of words, structure, imagery, and feeling—that are more easily overlooked in standard typography. The central and dominating position of the verb that governs the six verses, for example, is stressed by placing it in the apex of the triangle. In the same way, the effect of descent is heightened by making "desnuda" stand alone over the center space of the inner triangle as the reader's eye shifts to the bottom left corner of the triangle to read the second couplet. The metaphor of moon-woman is actually multiple: moon-well = woman-eyes, hence well = eyes. Where this multiplicity might be overlooked if read in standard (vertical) form, it is inescapable when the two couplets are placed side by side in the base of the triangle. In the same way, the commonality of "Baja / desnuda" to the multiple metaphor of the other two couplets is also dramatically obvious. The total effect is a greater clarity and expressiveness of the poet's sentiment in writing the poem and of the reader's re-creation of that sentiment.

A similar analysis can be applied to "Retrato" ["Portrait"], with its capitalized word in the center:

Al mirarme   a mí
                         TÚ
te miras   a ti

[When looking at   me
                         YOU
look at   yourself]

The graphic arrangement stresses the central place of the beloved not only in the poem but in the poet's life. Moreover, the form suggests a vertical reading of "Al mirarme / te miras," either with or without the emphasis of the central pronoun. The reader is also invited to read the right-hand column vertically in the same way, which since it does not stand alone syntactically, becomes an echo of the column on the left. The total effect, which would be lost in the standard arrangement, is that of "TÚ" as the center of a system that governs the relationship with the other words. Finally, the merging of "yo" and "tú," the theme of the poem, is heightened by the arrangement of the words.

In "Adivinanza en forma de octágono" ["Riddle in Octagonal Form"] the possibilities of interpretation are multiplied through the various combinations of linear relationships. The reader is instructed to place the numbered phrases on the eight lines that intersect at the center, an obvious device to maximize his participation in the re-creation of the poem. The immediate effect is the completion of the pairs through logical extension of the original statement: "Tú en el centro / Este y Oeste Norte y Sur." Once read in couplets, the eight verses can be read in their original unpaired order (from 1 through 8) with more meaning. Furthermore, the intersection of the lines suggests restatements of the same idea. There is no doubt, at least, that all participate in the common center, which must symbolize a source of life. More than the octagonal form, the innovation here is the invitation to perceive the numerous possibilities fulfilled by the poem. In this sense, it suggests a larger view of poetry's power in man's life.

"Vuelta" ["Return"] like so many of Paz's titles, has a double meaning. In its most obvious sense, developed from an epigraph by López Velarde,[3] it is the poet's return to his native Mexico City after an absence. He views the city through the points of view of memory and fresh observation, comparing what it was with what it seems today, fearing for its future. Anyone who has visited the Mexican capital and returned, after even a relatively short interval, will understand the nature of Paz's experience. In a more symbolic sense the title refers to the circular structure of the poem itself, in which the final stanza views the same setting described in the first, indicating to the reader that the circle has been closed ("He vuelto adonde empecé" [I have gone back to where I began]). The comparison between the two, and the philosophical implications of the conclusion, are an integral part of the poem's theme.

In the first of the seven stanzas the poet lists the impressions he receives as he walks through the streets, recounting in impersonal terms the sounds and objects that he perceives. Although he is conscious of himself in the setting ("Estoy en Mixcoac"), he draws no conclusions and makes no judgment, except to comment at the end of the stanza on the vertiginous effects of memory. This impressionistic painting of the city is uniformly pleasant, dominated by light and sound. Even the single note of disorder in this stanza ("En los buzones / se pudren las cartas" [Letters rot / in the mailboxes]) has a picturesque tone suggestive of leisure rather than neglect. Occasional use of surrealistic imagery ("Tiempo / tendido a secar en las azoteas" [Time / stretched to dry on the roof tops]) heightens the effect of a postcard scene.

The second stanza provides the affective commentary that is lacking in the first, excluding now almost all observation of external reality, with the possible exception of the final observation. Although the second verse refers to the poet's feelings ("estoy rodeado de ciudad" [I am surrounded by city]), it is only a framework. The poet feels himself becoming insubstantial as he loses first his body and then his spirit. Exactly in the center of the stanza is "Mediodía / puño de luz que golpea y golpea" [Noon / pounding fist of light], which is the opposite of the gentle and attractive light of the first stanza. As the poet speculates casually on what it might be like to die in an office or on the pavement, a passerby becomes as insubstantial as he has felt himself to be. Here the reader of other poems in which Paz sees himself in the act of seeing himself may well wonder if the passerby is not in fact the poet.

The third stanza is a vivid depiction of a suffering spirit—the lay version of a soul in hell. It is so generalized that it is not the poet's suffering nor any individual's, but rather the

abstract torment of all the city's inhabitants. The repeated
use of "en," which begins eleven of the stanza's eighteen
verses, suggests the breadth of feeling that is conveyed. Yet it
is at the same time a complex series of abstractions that are
the subjects: "germinación de pesadillas" [germination of
nightmares], "impalpables poblaciones del deseo" [desire's
ghost population], and "pululación de ideas con uñas y col-
millos" [teeming clawed tusked ideas]. Solitude and emp-
tiness create a spiritual desert in which suffering is the
natural climate.

An allusion in the fourth verse is a minor but interesting
example of the difficulties presented to Paz's readers:

> Germinación de pesadillas
> infestación de imágenes leprosas
> en el vientre los sesos los pulmones
> en el sexo del templo y del colegio

> [Germination of nightmares
> infestation of leprous images
> in the belly brains lungs
> in the genitals of the college and the temple]

Schoolboy sex, of course, is readily apprehensible, but "el
sexo del templo" is puzzling. Its point of origin for the poet is
inadvertently revealed in his interview with Rita Guibert, in
which he traces the development of his early atheism:

> Era oligatorio asistir a misa, y las misas se celebraban en
> una capilla muy bonita: el colegio era un edificio de
> fines del siglo XVIII o principios del XIX que antes había
> sido una hacienda. Las misas eran largas, los sermones
> aburridos y mi fe comenzó a congelarse. Me aburría y
> esto era ya una blasfemia porque me daba cuenta que me
> aburría. Además pensaba en las muchachas. La Iglesia se
> convirtió en una proveedora de sueños eróticos cada vez
> más indecentes.[4]

[Attendance at mass was obligatory, and the masses took place in a very pretty chapel: the school was a late 18th or early 19th century building that had been a hacienda. The masses were long, the sermons boring, and my faith began to cool. I was bored and that was already a blasphemy because I realized that I was bored. Moreover, I thought about girls. The Church became a provider of increasingly indecent erotic daydreams.]

With the biographical origin in mind, the reader understands the allusion perfectly. Without it, he is left to create his own relationship between the concepts of church and sex. Perhaps it is only the latter possibility that the poet intended.

Just as Paz's masterpiece, *Piedra de sol*, alternates analysis of individual agony with a vision of a sick society, so here in the fourth stanza he portrays the consequences for the city (and therefore for the nation) of the generalized agony of individuals. The stanza constitutes a list of current and future enemies of civilization. Through a series of ferociously critical symbols, the poet flays the economists, the politicians, the militarists, and the planners, all of whom have put selfish interests above service to others. The fifth stanza is an extension of the fourth, with the emphasis now not on the types of people who prevent a harmonious society, but on the wasteland that they have created. The miserable shanty towns are only the most obvious image of a misery that is "costurones de cicatrices / callejas en carne viva" [thoroughfares of scars / valleys of living flesh]. The analogy of the suffering body of the city with the illness of the individual spirit of the third stanza is clear. The climactic commentary of the final verse ("Ciudad / montón de palabras rotas" [City / heap of broken words]) contains a dual diagnosis of doom: the broken words are not only broken promises but the failures of communication.

The latter is the subject of the brief sixth stanza, an eloquent protest against the lack of a common language. Paz here laments, as he has so often in his essays, particularly in *El arco y la lira*, the disappearance of what he calls "comunión," here symbolized by Aztec society. The center, the axis around which the community used to move and ought to move, has been replaced by the isolated person whose suffering is portrayed in the third stanza. The sign of that fragmentation, which is also implied to be its cause, is the dollar sign stamped on every forehead.

The introductory phrase ("Estamos rodeados" [We are surrounded]) of the final stanza, then, has as one of its meanings the feeling of siege, bewilderment, and frustration. Looking to the poem's point of origin, and the negative attitude that has prevailed and become intensified after the first stanza, the poet wonders how to evaluate his experience. Once again, the reader participates in the creation of the poem. The answer, according to the Chinese sage whom the poet quotes, is that it is an error to judge in terms of success or failure: "Todo es ganancia / si todo es pérdida" [All is gain / if all is lost]. The epigraph's interpretation of a lost Eden is erroneous; the only meaning of the trees, the fountains, and the light and shadows that comprise the beatific vision of the first stanza, now recalled here, is whatever one may wish to assign it in one's personal recollection. It had, and has, no meaning outside the poem, as the poem has no meaning outside the reader. The effect of the concluding verses is not only to erase the lines between poet and reader and between imagination and reality, but also to abolish the experience of linear time: both past and present are equally inaccessible to efforts to categorize and to understand the world. The most we can achieve, the poet implies, is partial comprehension of the poetic process and its magic in restoring us to ourselves, the original return of the title.

The theme of the final stanza is a denial not only of the circumstances that produce the poem, but also of the poem itself. The implied answer to the question of verse 3 is simply that the question has no meaning. If "Los lugares son confluencias / aleteo de presencias" [Places are confluences / flutters of beings], then reality is not ultimately definable in the poem, and the poem can never be complete. Its justification is simply that it poses questions that cannot be answered. The theme that joins the intensely personal with the universal also serves as the common background of the section titled "Confluencias" ["Junctions"], with the notable difference that their full comprehension depends in great part on some familiarity with the work of the various painters, writers, and the photographer to whom they are dedicated. "Objetos y apariciones" ["Objects and Apparitions"], in praise of Joseph Cornell, is typical of the way in which Paz employs his personal vision to involve the reader in an exploration similar to Cornell's.[5]

The theme of the poem, summarized in its title, is the contrast of something solid,tangible, and "real" (the objects), with the vagueness, imagination, and variability of subjective reality (the appearances). Each stanza contains at least one element, frequently stated in a single verse, that leads the reader to philosophical speculation, what might be called a window on infinity. The structure of the poem, therefore, is more a theme with variations than a development in which the theme grows organically from an initial statement through a progression of changes to a logical conclusion.

The first three stanzas have an identical form in which the first two verses consist of realistic descriptions of Cornell's style, followed by a verse expressing their effect on the poet, who sees them in terms of absolute or timeless values. In the fourth stanza, the procedure is reversed by giving the first verse the poet's personal reaction, with a tension created by the impersonality of "Memoria teje" [Memory weaves] and the personal action (and reaction) of "y destejo los ecos" [And I unweave the echoes]. In the fifth stanza the window of infinity is replaced by a reality within (or beyond) reality, supplied by the perceptivity of the viewer who can discern "El fuego enterrado en el espejo, / el agua dormida en el ágata" [Fire buried in the mirror, / water sleeping in the agate]. Since the same kind of implication, as opposed to statement, is found in the tenth stanza, the poem can be considered to be loosely organized in parts of five stanzas

each, with a concluding section of four. Each of the stanzas in
the poem, whether through a surrealistic interpretation (as in
stanza 11), or the poet's philosphical reaction (as in stanzas 6,
8, 9, and 12) broadens the meaning beyond that revealed by
the viewer's first reaction.

The initial verse of the eleventh stanza reveals the effec-
tiveness of Paz's identification with Cornell's objectives. In
the metaphor of the comb being played like a harp, Paz drama-
tizes the comparison by drawing the first element from the
"real" world; by reversing the order of *peine* and *harpa*, one
sees that the "logical" order diminishes the success with
which the poem creates a vivid and unclassifiable reality.

The progression of the subjects of the last four stanzas
underscores the progression from reality to super-reality and
reveals the significance of the contrast stated by the poem's
title. The tableau of the eleventh stanza is given meaning by
the poet's personal interpretation, which is unlikely to be
shared in precisely the same way by any other viewer. In the
following stanza, he looks not at the tableau for meaning but
to his own reaction in the poem. His conclusion about
whether reality rests on objects or their appearances and
transformations, is, typically, paradoxical: the apparitions are
both "patentes" and ephemeral. The final stanza, an *envoi* in
the form of a couplet, represents not only a commentary on
the nature of poetry, but a fulfillment for the poet who has
been successful in capturing it for at least a moment. Yet the
terminal emphasis of "un instante" suggests that "Objetos y
apariciones" lapses into silence.

"Nocturno de San Ildefonso" ["San Ildefonso Nocturne"]
is among the freest and least structured poems of *Vuelta*, and
therefore one of the most hermetic. Yet because of these
characteristics, it also reveals both the poet's subjects and his
approaches to them in the most recent stage of his develop-
ment. Written in free verses of irregular length, this long
poem is divided into four unequal sections. The first, which
is also the shortest, has the function of introduction as it
develops the subject of a night scene announced by the title.
To this clearly defined subject is added the implied and more

significant one of the poet's creativity, the familiar awareness
of himself creating the poem. This awareness becomes appar-
ent at the beginning of the second stanza ("Signos-semi-
llas: / la noche los dispara" [Sign-seeds / the night shoots
them off]), and is continued at once in the form of "lumbres
divagantes, / racimos de sílabas" [rambling sparks / syllable
clusters].

In both the stated subject of night and the implied subject
of poetry, Paz senses the existence of a reality behind ap-
pearances. This super-reality (which may not be the ultimate)
is suggested in the agent of the initial verb: it is not the poet
who invents the night in his window but another night. In
fact, all of the impersonally generated actions are related to
the basic metaphors of fireworks, whose mover is identified
only in the final verse of the second stanza as the city itself.

When the poet enters the poem with a personal verb at the
beginning of the third stanza ("Estoy a la entrada de un túnel"
[I am at the entrance to a tunnel]), the reality of his own
existence is also subordinated to another reality, revealed in
his questioning of his identity through a paradoxical double
location: he is simultaneously at the beginning and end of a
tunnel created by phrases that puncture time. Furthermore,
he (and therefore his work) are subject to the will of someone
who, at the section's conclusion, expresses his will through
the new reality that the night invented in the first verse. The
effect of this unknown creator's efforts is analogous to an
illness from which the poet suffers, expressed by symptoms
of emptiness, dizziness, and chills. In contrast to the chills
are the swarms of burning words (recalling the metaphor of
fireworks) and the insistence of the night which, now person-
ified but still unknown, "palpa mis pensamientos" [touches
my thoughts]. The concluding "¿Qué quiere?" is a transition
to the second section, which the reader expects will be at
least a partial answer to the question.

At first reading, the second section does not seem to sup-
ply a direct answer to the question regarding the poet's rela-
tionship to the world. The reality described here—a city
scene in 1931 (first stanza), a glimpse of the city's history

(stanzas 2 and 3), and recollections of youthful dialogue and debates—is essentially external to the poet's concerns of the first section. It is, furthermore, described objectively, so that it lacks the anguish that colors the introduction. In this sense, the first two sections portray the same kind of contrast that we noted earlier in the two halves of *Piedra de sol:* the first turns inward, looking to the poet's feelings for a definition of reality; the second turns outward, attempting to find meaning in the description of what was seen and heard.

On a closer reading of the second section, the reader sees its connection with the first in the implication that reality outside the poet continues to attempt to communicate with him. The idea of a reality underlying appearances, and in fact controlling them, is conveyed by the streetlights that invent "unreal pools of yellowish light" (recalling the fragments invented and erased by the city in the first section) and the apparitions whose source is divided time. The fact that all of the youthful recollections terminate, in the last four lines of the section, with a return to the poem confirms the impression that these memories derive, paradoxically, from an outside source. They are the message that the night has sent to the poet.

The consciousness of creating the poem is not only the link between the second and third sections, but the recurrent theme of the entire poem. The poem—and poetry in general—has the magical quality of abolishing time. In the same way that the poet saw himself earlier at both ends of the tunnel, so he views himself here in two contexts of time, as the young man who is the poem's subject and as the mature man who writes the poem—and is also the poem's subject. The place referred to ("Aquí encarnan / los espectros amigos, / las ideas se disipan" [Here the friendly ghosts / become flesh, / ideas dissolve]) is more the concept of poetry than the route of the walk. Poetry changes the perception of reality as well as of time, as seen in two opposing transformations: ghosts become flesh, and the solidity of ideas vanishes.

Since the second and third stanzas deal respectively with youthful political consciousness and the concept of history, the subthemes of the third section are similar to those of the second. The order here, however, is exactly the opposite of the second, which proceeded from history through politics to poetry. Thus Paz avoids restatement by reversing the flow of association. The position of poetry, at the beginning and end of both series, indicates its thematic dominance.

In the third section, the poet contrasts history, which is a human concept, with truth, which lies outside time, words, and man himself. In a quadruple metaphor (time, sun, stones, and words), he attempts to convey the complexities of truth after the introductory declaration that "La verdad / es el fondo del tiempo sin historia" [Truth / is the base of time without history]. The reader acquainted with Paz's work is not surprised that the metaphor begins with a paradox ("El peso / del instante que no pesa" [The weight / of the weightless moment]) or that the following verse recalls the title of *Piedra de sol.* The metaphor extends the meanings of time to timelessness and of sun (which is also timeless) to an illumination of words. Together they comprise the evidence of truth ("Oculto, inmóvil, intocable" [Hidden, immobile, untouchable]) that is the present moment, which is differentiated from the illusion of its "presencias."

The final stanza of this section makes a further comparison of truth, history, and poetry. Poetry is not truth but the "resurreción de las presencias." Like history, it is made by man; unlike history it enables man to see through opposites to a meaning beyond meaning. It is, therefore, the "puente colgante entre historia y verdad" [suspension bridge between history and truth], and man is held by it from falling into the void. This stanza, then, is another fragment not so much of Paz's praise of poetry, but of his *ars poetica.* Once again we find the extension of the Surrealist credo in which poetry is defined as the magic that is central to man's existence.

The fourth section is introduced by a restatement of verse 8 of the third section's first stanza: "Las ideas se disipan, / quedan los espectros" [Ideas scatter, / the ghosts remain]. Truth, time, and language are referred to again, but in an imprecise way that seems separated from the embracing con-

clusions of the previous section. The second stanza returns to
the scene of the night sky, which recalls the beginning of the
poem and suggests circularity of structure at the same time
that the poet glimpses behind "apenas visibles, / las con-
stelaciones verdaderas" [barely visible, the true constel-
lations].

The sight of the moon introduces the subject of the poet's
sleeping wife and the theme of her beauty, which is developed
as a self-contained reality. The connection between his ide-
alized vision of her and the previous section is established by
the conclusion of the penultimate stanza:

> La verdad
> es el oleaje de una respiración
> y las visiones que miran unos ojos cerrados:
> palpable misterio de la persona.
>
> [*Poemas*, 639]

> [Truth
> is the swell of a breath
> and the visions closed eyes see:
> the palpable mystery of the person.]

The concluding stanza really is not a conventional con-
clusion. As dawn brings to the poet thoughts about the nature
of dying, he concentrates on the moonlit figure of his wife.
The final verses suggest the continuation of movement
rather than a cessation. In that sense, the poem simply stops
rather than ends. The entire fourth section, in fact, is an
epilogue to the philosophical conclusions of the third sec-
tion. Its function is not to advance those conclusions but to
dramatize the poet's perception of the truth of the present
moment, which, he acknowledges, cannot be adequately de-
fined in words. Again, the poet suggests that the real con-
clusion of the poem is in the mind of the reader.

Surveying all of the compositions of *Vuelta*, one can dis-
cern a line of development that marks the transition from
Pasado en claro to what might be in other poets the limits of
poetic expression. All of the poems of the first section,

"Configuraciones," continue the subject of *Pasado en claro*, the writing of the poem. The remaining compositions, however, taken as a group, seek to go beyond the text to what can only be called the unwritten poem. Paz's objective reveals itself particularly in the dispersion of the final verses of the other sections. Rather than a return to the hermeticism of his earlier poetry, this fragmentation represents a dramatic attempt to advance the possibilities of poetry beyond conventional limits. Paz's efforts to define himself, love, poetry, and the world began with the freedom offered to him by language; after thousands of verses, he now has reached the frontier of poetic texts. Perhaps the greatest gift that he bestows on the reader, in addition to the record of his own struggle and hopes, is the realization that every man carries the potential for poetic feeling and expression.

8 Conclusion

Although the stages of Paz's development studied here cannot be reduced to an exclusivity for each of his books, a broad view of their achievements reveals a progressively complex role for the reader. Whether such a role conforms to the poet's conscious intentions is open to question. In fact, judging from the combination of techniques within books and even within poems, one may wonder whether Paz thinks in personal terms of the text's reception. To see an evolution of demands imposed by the major poems, therefore, is a function of criticism rather than of poetic creativity.

Piedra de sol, in its subjects, tone, and imagery, is a continuum of much of the poetry published before 1957, collected in *Libertad bajo palabra*. It's length, unity, and structure, however, constitute an innovation. The most obvious structural feature—and the most widely commented on by critics—is the circularity of repeating the introductory lines as the conclusion. What has frequently been overlooked is the effect on one's perception of time caused by the rereading. That effect is complicated by the tension between the two halves of the poem, which also anticipates the polarities of *Ladera este:* the individual and society, the subjective and the objective, frustration and fulfillment, fragmentation and integration. A deeper and more personal reaction to the poem results not only from the recollection of the tension between the halves, but also from the growing awareness of their similarities.

The structure of *Piedra de sol* does not fuse with the theme (as it does later in *Pasado en claro*), but reinforces it: the poet's search is symbolic of everyone's. By incorporating historical subjects in the second part, Paz broadens the geography and the chronology of his audience's perspective, so that the text becomes universal in its implication.

In *Salamandra* the poet abandons the relationship between structure and theme to explore ways in which the latter is created by intensive development of the subject. His technique in this approach is to concentrate on the subject and to be inexplicit about the theme. In fact, the first reaction on concluding a poem of *Salamandra* may be to question whether there is a theme. The variety of interpretations of these poems may well be greater than that of any other book by Paz, demonstrating that bewilderment can be used as the first step to determine the text's significance. The subject reappears in many guises, so that the poet implies that he will not make a final choice about meaning. The response to questions about the theme, accordingly, must come from a source outside the text.

In *Blanco* Paz returns to his emphasis on structure, organized spatially in multiple parts. The emphasis in this poem is on the complexity of relationships among the many parts of the poem, indicated in the prefatory suggestions for reading it. The combinations of single- and double-column strophes constitute numerous separate poems that connect in different ways to each other and to the poem as a whole. The significance of the poet's instructions is the liberty given to the reader to combine the subordinate poems in different ways, as if they were modules that an architect might apply to achieve various options in design. Although the options have a limit, the poet's list is not exhaustive. By omitting several ways of reading the poem, he provides an incentive to imagination and sensitivity, and—what is particularly important for understanding the last two books studied here—a sense of participation.

Blanco also adumbrates *Pasado en claro* and *Vuelta* in taking its own composition as a theme. Unlike the later works, however, the poem is based on multiple construction, so that it has no single theme, but rather three: writing, love, and four approaches to reality that can be grouped as phenomenology. In this way writing is an element of the poem's complexity that must be considered equal in importance to the other two. The poem's success derives from the balance of their relationship rather than from the dominance of one theme.

In *Ladera este* Paz once again abandons structural complexity in order to challenge his audience by concentrating on a single element. In contrast to *Salamandra*, in which the subject is emphasized and the theme only implied, here the themes are fully formulated and presented as paradoxes. Under the influence of Buddhism, but following perceptions that date from the earliest poems of *Libertad bajo palabra*, the poet expresses the duality of reality. *Ladera este*, more than the balance of opposites, represents their interaction. Life and death, the self and the world, significance and emptiness, expression and nonexpression are the twin faces of his themes. The entire book can be seen as the expansion of one of the poet's favorite devices, the paradox, to the level of theme. The struggle of opposites and the need to reconcile them are so intense that the poem calls for a response to the questions that it raises.

Pasado en claro represents a further narrowing of the gap between the poet and the reader. Its innovation, like that of *Salamandra*, rests on the relationship between subject and theme rather than on structure. With this subject, the poet's reconstruction of his life and its meaning, the universality of the theme grows in proportion to the personal nature of its source. The essence of the autobiography revealed in the poem is the poet's effort to achieve expression in general and in this poem in particular. The subject, then, is the composition of the poem itself. What was one of several themes in *Blanco* becomes here all-embracing.

That theme, however, remains incomplete in the text—or, rather, open. At the level of personal history, the poet's work is unfinished because he cannot see it in its totality. At a more philosophical level, the theme of *Pasado en claro* is open because the poet refuses to conclude it. Only the response to the poem can express its final significance. It is, therefore, designed to be, like the achievements of Mallarmé and Duchamp, a scaffolding rather than a building. It is an "aparato de significar."

Vuelta should be viewed not as a work apart but as the

culmination of Paz's efforts to broaden the reactions and the responsibilities of the reader. The poems of this volume, in spite of their apparent diversity, share the purpose of stimulating individual responses to the text. What is apparent here is the intensity of the stimulus, so that in the silence created by the poem the reader is not invited but required to complete it. Since the character of that response necessarily varies, the nature of poetry itself is modified: Paz has converted his audience into poets. One wonders after reading *Vuelta* what Paz's trajectory will be in the future. There is implied in this book a philosophical and esthetic end of the line. Where can poetry go after reaching silence? The poet's inventiveness will no doubt solve this problem, just as he went beyond previous works, each of which could also have been considered the end of the line. Whatever course he takes, he will undoubtedly continue to carry out his mission, not so much of making poetry live or of living poetry, but of causing people to feel that they can make poems of their lives.

Notes

1. Introduction

1. The biographical section of this introduction is based on Alfredo Roggiano's "Persona y ámbito de Octavio Paz" (in *Octavio Paz* [Madrid: Editorial Fundamentos, 1979]), which utilizes interviews with Paz published by Guibert and Ríos.
2. Roggiano, "Persona y ámbito," 21-30.
3. Octavio Paz, *Ladera este (1962-1968)* (Mexico: Joaquín Mortiz, 1969), 173.
4. Ruth Needleman, "Poetry and the Reader," *Books Abroad*, 46 (1972), 553.
5. Ibid., 554, 556, and 559.
6. Gordon Brotherston, *Latin American Poetry: Origins and Presence* (Cambridge: Cambridge Univ. Press, 1975), 145.
7. Octavio Paz, *Apariencia desnuda* (Mexico: Ediciones Era, 1973), 77-78.
8. Gabriel Zaid, "Significaciones últimas," *La cultura en México*, 287 (16 Aug. 1967), 6.

2. *Piedra de sol:* The Divided Circle

1. José Emilio Pacheco, "Descripción de 'Piedra de sol,' " *Revista iberoamericana*, 37 (1971), 146.
2. Rachel Phillips, *The Poetic Modes of Octavio Paz* (London: Oxford Univ. Press, 1972), 17-18.
3. Pere Gimferrer, *Lecturas de Octavio Paz* (Barcelona: Editorial Anagrama, 1980), 47.
4. Phillips, *Poetic Modes*, 21.
5. Gérard de Nerval, *Les Chimères*, ed. Jeanine Moulin (Lille: Librairie Giard, 1949), 54-55.
6. François Constans, "Sophie Aurélia Artémis," *Mercure de*

France, 312 (1951), 270; Jean Richer, *Gérard de Nerval et les doctrines ésotériques* (Paris: Editions du Griffon d'or, 1947), 114.

7. The number thirteen, in addition to its traditional association with bad luck, has a specific application in the tarot cards, in which it connotes death (see Jean Onimus, "Artémis ou le ballet des heures," *Mercure de France*, 324 (1955), 74.) Thirteen is not only the hour of death, but also the lunar principle in general and the thirteen lunar months in particular. An illustration of Isis in one of Nerval's primary sources, Athanasius Kircher's *Oedipus aegyptiacus* (1652), seems to be connected concretely with Nerval's sonnet: "Ce chiffre de *treize* noms peut se rapporter au vers initial d'*Artémis* . . . . 'La treizième' c'est la *Lune* dans cette liste et le nom de Diane-Artémis (titre du sonnet de Nerval) constitue le pivot: il est précédé de six noms et suivi de six autres. Des correspondances aussi curieuses ne peuvent être dues au simple hasard (Richer, *Gérard de Nerval*, 119 and 128]. [This group of *thirteen* names can be applied to the initial verse of "Artémis." . . . . "The thirteenth" is the *Moon* in this list, and the name of Diana-Artemis (the title of Nerval's sonnet) constitutes the axis: it is preceded by six names and followed by six others. Such interesting relationships cannot be attributed to simple chance].

8. Onimus, "Artémis," 76.

9. In his *Les métamorphoses du cercle* (Paris: Plon, 1961), Georges Poulet describes the lengthy tradition of the circle in literature, and dedicates an entire chapter to Nerval. It is interesting to note that the only Spanish-speaking writer who merits such attention is Jorge Guillén.

10. François Constans, "Artémis ou les fleurs du désespoir," *Revue de litterature comparée*, 14 (1934), 362.

11. Richer, *Gérard de Nerval*, 126-27.

12. Octavio Paz, *El laberinto de la soledad* (Mexico: Fondo de Cultura Económica, 1959), 25.

13. Ibid. Emphasis his.

14. Jacques Soustelle, *La pensée cosmologique des anciens mexicains* (Paris: Hermann & Cie., 1940), 58.

15. Ibid., 85.

16. Ibid., 59.

17. Ibid., 62.

18. Ibid., 67.

19. By using the same verses as conclusion and introduction, Paz adapts to modern verse the principle of repetition (although not the versification) of the French *rondel* or *rondeau*. In its use of the colon, however, *Piedra de sol* actually begins the circle of text again instead of recalling it.

3. *Salamandra:* The Subject Itself

1. Ramón Xirau, *Octavio Paz: El sentido de la palabra* (Mexico: Joaquín Mortiz, 1970), 87-91.
2. Pliny *Natural History,* bk. 10, ch. 86 (Loeb Classical Library, 3, 413).
3. "Después que hubieron salido ambos sobre la tierra estuvieron quedos, sin moverse de un lugar el sol y la luna; y los dioses otra vez se hablaron, y dijeron: '¿Cómo podemos vivir? ¿No se menea el sol? ¡Hemos de vivir entre los villanos? Murámos todos y hagámosle que resucite por nuestra muerte.' Y luego el aire se encargó de matar a todos los dioses y matólos; y dícese que uno llamada *Xólotl* rehusaba la muerte, y dijo a los dioses. '¡Oh dioses! ¡No muera yo!' Y lloraba en gran manera, de suerte que se le hincharon los ojos de llorar; y cuando llegó a él el que mataba echó a huir, y escondiose entre los maizales, y convirtiose en pie de maíz, que tiene dos cañas, y los labradores le llaman *xólotl;* y fue visto y hallado entre los pies del maíz; otra vez echó a huir, y se escondió entre los magueyes, y convirtiose en maguey que tiene dos cuerpos que se llama *mexólotl;* otra vez fue visto, y echó a huir y metióse en el agua, y hízose pez que se llama *axólotl,* y de allí le tomaron y le mataron. Y dicen que aunque fueron muertos los dioses, no por eso se movió el sol, y luego el viento comenzó a soplar y ventear reciamente, y él le hizo moverse para que anduviese su camino; y después que el sol comenzó a caminar la luna se estuvo queda en el lugar donde estaba. Después del sol, comenzó la luna a andar; de esta manera se desviaron el uno del otro y así salen en diversos tiempos, el sol dura un día, y la luna trabaja en la noche, o alumbra en la noche" (Bernardino de Sahagún, *Historia general de las cosas de Nueva España* [México: Robredo, 1938], 2, 260).

4. *Blanco:* Multiple Meanings

1. Gimferrer, *Lecturas,* 61-62.
2. Ibid., 62.
3. Xirau, *Octavio Paz,* 91-93.
4. Jean Franco, "'¡Oh mundo por poblar, hoja en blanco!" *Revista iberoamericana,* 37 (1972), 160.
5. Guillermo Sucre, " 'Blanco': Un archipiélago de signos," in Angel Flores, ed., *Aproximaciones a Octavio Paz* (Mexico: Joaquín Mortiz, 1974), 232-36.
6. Enrique Pezzoni, " 'Blanco': La respuesta al deseo," in Angel Flores, ed., *Aproximaciones a Octavio Paz* (Mexico: Joaquín Mortiz, 1974), 237-53.
7. Only the first edition utilizes color.

8. See particularly Manuel Durán, "El impacto del Oriente en la obra de Octavio Paz," in Roggiano, *Octavio Paz*, 173-204; and Diego Martínez Torrón, "Octavio Paz en el contexto de Oriente," in Keith McDuffie and Alfredo Roggiano, eds., *Texto/Contexto en la literatura iberoamericana* (Madrid: n.p., 1980), 203-14.

9. Wallace Fowlie's commentary on the sonnet "Ses purs ongles" reveals the similarity between its theme and that of *Blanco*. "Ses purs ongles is a sonnet of exceptional poetic rigour. It provides the picture of a void reflecting the universe. In the profoundest sense, it is a poem about poetry, about the power and the plenitude of speech. The final image of the septet of constellations mounting in the sky is analogous to the mounting of words to the consciousness of the poet, or the renascence of the idea" (*Mallarmé* [Chicago: Univ. of Chicago Press, 1953], 80).

10. Octavio Paz, *Los signos en rotación* (Buenos Aires: Sur, 1965), 42 and 44.

11. Ibid., 43.

12. Ibid., 23-24.

13. Ibid., 69-70.

14. Ibid., 63.

15. Ibid., 62.

16. Octavio Paz, *Conjunciones y disyunciones* (Mexico: Joaquín Mortiz, 1969), 43-44.

17. Gimferrer, *Lecturas*, 70.

5. *Ladera este*: Polarities

1. Xirau, *Octavio Paz*, 107-8.

2. This poem, first published separately in 1965, was grouped with others under the heading "Hacia el comienzo" in *Ladera este*. In *Poemas* that group is separated from another headed by the volume's title.

3. Paz's affinity for this contemporary American composer suggests their mutual goals and techniques, particularly the positive values assigned to silence. As a pioneer in electronic music, Cage was criticized for being "destructive"; his intention was said to be "to save music from itself by removing its narcotic qualities and its personalized pretentiousness, as well as all identifiable structure and rhetoric." See *Contemporary Authors*, 1st rev. (Detroit, Mich.: Gale Research Co., 1975), 13-16, 131-32. The authoritative *New Grove Dictionary* states simply that "he has had a greater impact on world music than any other American composer of the 20th century."

4. Philip Rawson, *Tantra: The Indian Cult of Ecstasy* (New York: Avon, 1973), 8.

5. Ibid., 9-12.

6. Ibid., 14.

7. Ruth Needleman, in "Poetry and the Reader," *Books Abroad*, 46 (1972), 550-59, provides an interesting evolution of the concept of the reader through Paz's statements about poetry.

6. *Pasado en claro:* The Poem Itself

1. Jean Liscano, "Lectura libre de un libro de poesía de Octavio Paz," in Roggiano, *Octavio Paz*, 347, 349, 352-57.

2. Gimferrer, *Lecturas*, 73-83.

3. José Miguel Oviedo, "Los pasos de la memoria: Lectura de un poema de Octavio Paz," *Revista de occidente*, 14 (1976), 42-44 and 51. I am greatly indebted to this thorough and perceptive analysis.

4. The version in *Poemas* extensively revises the first edition (1975).

5. Oviedo, "Pasos," 43.

6. Claire Céa, *Octavio Paz* (Paris: P. Seghers, 1965).

7. Oviedo, "Pasos," 44.

8. Ibid., 46.

9. See note 3 above. This section of the poem was added after the publication of Oviedo's article.

10. Oviedo, "Pasos," 48.

11. Ibid., 49.

12. Whether Oviedo (49) is correct in deducing that language and air are merged in one subject is something that each reader must determine. The beginning of the fourteenth section strengthens his interpretation.

13. Oviedo, "Pasos," 50. His line numbers refer to the first edition of the poem. It is interesting to note that Paz, who makes no secret of his youthful rejection of religion, corrected "Dios" so that it appears with a small letter in subsequent editions.

14. Ibid., 51. Emphasis his.

15. Ramón Xirau, "Pasado en claro," *La gaceta*, 62 (Feb. 1976), 8.

16. Octavio Paz, *Apariencia desnuda. La obra de Marcel Duchamp* (Mexico: Ediciones Era, 1973), 15-20, 29-30.

17. Ibid., 19-20 and 29-30.

18. Ibid., 36. See also 33-35.

19. Paz, *Los signos en rotación*, 44-45.

20. Paz, *Apariencia desnuda*, 77 and 84. Emphasis his.

7. *Vuelta:* Toward Silence

1. Gimferrer's eloquent reading (*Lecturas,* 103-18) provides a detailed anlaysis of the reader's involvement as the poem develops from immobility to solidity and from one blank to another.

2. See my article on "The Mirror as Image and Theme in the Poetry of Octavio Paz," *Symposium,* 10 (1956), 251-70.

3. The first stanza of "El retorno maléfico."

4. Rita Guibert, *Siete voces,* 227-28; quoted in Roggiano, *Octavio Paz,* 6.

5. Joseph Cornell was an innovative American Surrealist artist whose popular success developed primarily after his death in 1972. Specializing in "found" objects, he arranged miniature tableaux in stage-like boxes to create worlds in which fantasy, memory, people, and objects are seen in often surprising juxtaposition.

Bibliography

Alazraki, Jaime. "Para una poética del silencio." *Cuadernos hispanoamericanos*, 115 (1979), 157-84.

Alonso, Amado. *Materia y forma en poesía.* Madrid: Gredos, 1955.

Armand, Octavio. "Viento entero." In *Aproximaciones a Octavio Paz*, edited by Angel Flores. Mexico: Joaquín Mortiz, 1974. 209-27.

Balakian, Anna. "Sounds Walking over Silence." *Review,* 6 (Fall 1972), 15-17.

Brotherston, Gordon. *Latin American Poetry: Origins and Presence.* Cambridge: Cambridge Univ. Press, 1975.

Burland, C.A. *The Gods of Mexico.* New York: G.P. Putnam's Sons, 1967.

Caso, Alfonso. *Los calendarios prehispánicos.* Mexico: Universidad Autónoma de México, 1967.

Céa, Claire. *Octavio Paz.* Paris: P. Seghers, 1965.

Constans, François. "Artémis ou les fleurs du désespoir." *Revue de litterature comparée,* 14 (1934), 337-71.

———. "Sophie Aurélia Artémis." *Mercure de France,* 312 (1951), 267-81.

Debicki, Andrew. "El trasfondo filosófico y la experiencia poética en obras de Octavio Paz." In *Poetas hispanoamericanos contemporáneos.* Madrid: Gredos, 1976. 141-58.

D'Harnoncourt, Anne. "The Absence and Necessity of Meaning." *Review,* 6 (Fall 1972), 18-21.

Durán, Manuel. "La huella del Oriente en la poesía de Octavio Paz." *Revista iberoamericana,* 37 (1971), 97-116.

Embeita, María. "Entrevistas, Octavio Paz." *Insula,* 260-61 (July-Aug. 1968), 13.

Fein, John M., "La estructura de 'Piedra de sol.' " *Revista iberoamericana,* 38 (1972), 73-94.

————. "Himno entre ruinas." In *Aproximaciones a Octavio Paz,* edited by Angel Flores. Mexico: Joaquín Mortiz, 1974. 165-70.

————. "The Mirror as Image and Theme in the Poetry of Octavio Paz." *Symposium,* 10 (1956), 251-70.

Earle, Peter G., and Germán Gullón, eds. *Surrealismo / Surrealismos: Latinoamérica y España.* Philadelphia: Department of Romance Languages, Univ. of Pennsylvania, 1977.

Flores, Angel, ed. *Aproximaciones a Octavio Paz.* Mexico: Joaquín Mortiz, 1974.

Forrester, Viviane. "La Géographie mentale d'Octavio Paz." *La Quinzaine Littéraire,* 16-30 Sept. 1972, 13-14.

Fowlie, Wallace. *French Literature: Its History and Meaning.* Englewood Cliffs, N.J.: Prentice-Hall, 1973.

————. *Mallarmé.* Chicago: Univ. of Chicago Press, 1953.

Franco, Jean. *An Introduction to Spanish American Literature.* Cambridge: Cambridge Univ. Press, 1969.

————. "¡Oh mundo por poblar, hoja en blanco!" *Revista iberoamericana,* 37 (1972), 226-42.

Fuente, Ovidio C. "Teoría poética de Octavio Paz." *Cuadernos americanos,* 31 (1972), 226-42.

Fuentes, Carlos. "El tiempo de Octavio Paz." In *Casa con dos puertas.* Mexico: Joaquín Mortiz, 1970. 151-57.

Gallagher, D.P. *Modern Latin American Literature.* London: Oxford Univ. Press, 1973.

Gimferrer, Pere. *Lecturas de Octavio Paz.* Barcelona: Editorial Anagrama, 1980.

Guibert, Rita. "Octavio Paz." In *Seven Voices: Seven Latin American Writers Talk to Rita Guibert.* New York: Knopf, 1973. 181-275. [Published in Spanish as *Siete voces.* Mexico: Editorial Novaro, 1974. 198-293.]

"Homage to Octavio Paz." *World Literature Today,* 56 (1982), 587-763.

"Homenaje a Octavio Paz." *Cuadernos hispanoamericanos,* 115, 343-45 (1979), 1-791.

"Interview: Octavio Paz." *Diacritics,* 2 (Fall 1972), 35-40.

Ivask, Ivar, ed. *The Perpetual Present: The Poetry and Prose of Octavio Paz.* Norman, Okla.: Univ. of Oklahoma Press, 1973.

Jonsson-Devillers, Edith. "Vueltas y revueltas a *Vuelta:* Esbozo para un análisis de la intertextualidad." In *Texto/Contexto en la literatura iberoamericana,* edited by Keith McDuffie and Alfredo Roggiano. Madrid: n.p., 1980. 155-62.

León-Portilla, Miguel. *Aztec Thought and Culture.* Norman, Okla.: Univ. of Oklahoma Press, 1963.

Lewis, Tom J. Review of *Renga: A Chain of Poems*, by Octavio Paz, Jacques Roubaud, Eduardo Sanguineti, and Charles Tomlinson. *Review*, 7 (Winter 1972), 61-62.

Liscano, Juan. "Lectura libre de un libro de poesía de Octavio Paz." In *Octavio Paz*, edited by Alfredo Roggiano. Madrid: Editorial Fundamentos, 1979. 347-60.

McDuffie, Keith, and Alfredo Roggiano, eds. *Texto / Contexto en la literatura iberoamericana*. Madrid: n.p., 1980.

Magis, Carlos H. *La poesía hermética de Octavio Paz*. Mexico: El Colegio de México, 1978.

Martínez Torrón, Diego, ed. *Octavio Paz: La búsqueda del comienzo; escritos sobre el surrealismo*. Madrid: Editorial Fundamentos, 1974.

Needleman, Ruth. "Hacia Blanco[sic]." *Revista iberoamericana*, 37 (1971), 177-81.

———. "Poetry and the Reader." *Books Abroad*, 46 (1972), 550-59.

Nerval, Gérard de. *Les Chimères*. Edited by Jeanine Moulin. Lille: Librairie Giard, 1949.

Onimus, Jean. "Artémis ou le ballet des heures." *Mercure de France*, 324 (1955), 73-76.

Ortega, Julio. " 'Viento entero': El tiempo en un día." In *Aproximaciones a Octavio Paz* edited by Angel Flores. Mexico: Joaquín Mortiz, 1974. 200-208.

Oviedo, José Miguel. "Los pasos de la memoria: Lectura de un poema de Octavio Paz." *Revista de occidente*, 14 (1976), 42-51.

———. "Return to the Beginning: Paz in His Recent Poetry." *World Literature Today*, 56 (1982), 612-18.

Pacheco, José Emilio. "Descripción de 'Piedra de sol.' " *Revista iberoamericana*, 37 (1971), 135-46.

Palau de Nemes, Graciela. "Blanco [sic] de Octavio Paz: Una mística espacialista." *Revista iberoamericana*, 37 (1971), 183-96.

Paz, Octavio. *Apariencia desnuda. La obra de Marcel Duchamp*. Mexico: Ediciones Era, 1973.

———. *El arco y la lira*. 3d ed. Mexico: Fondo de Cultura Económica, 1972.

———. *Blanco*. Mexico: Joaquín Mortiz, 1967.

———. *Children of the Mire: Modern Poetry from Romanticism to the Avant-Garde*. Cambridge, Mass.: Harvard Univ. Press, 1974.

———. *Configurations*. New York: New Directions, 1971.

———. *Conjunciones y disyunciones*. Mexico: Joaquín Mortiz, 1969.

———. *A Draft of Shadows and Other Poems*. New York: New Directions, 1979.

———. "Hablar y decir, leer y contemplar (segunda parte)." *Vuelta*, 64 (March 1982), 29-33.

———. *El laberinto de la soledad*. Mexico: Fondo de Cultura Económica, 1959.

———. *Ladera este (1962-1968)*. Mexico: Joaquín Mortiz, 1969.

———. *Libertad bajo palabra: Obra poética, 1937-1957*. 2d ed. Mexico: Fondo de Cultura Económica, 1960.

———. *Luna silvestre*. Mexico: Fábula, 1933.

———. *Pasado en claro*. Mexico: Fondo de Cultura Económica, 1975.

———. *Piedra de sol*. Mexico: Tezontle, 1957.

———. *Poemas: 1930-1975*. Barcelona: Seix Barral, 1979.

———. "Poesía de soledad y poesía de comunión." *El hijo pródigo*, 1 (1943), 271-78.

———. *Salamandra*. Mexico: Joaquín Mortiz, 1962.

———. *Los signos en rotación*. Buenos Aires: Sur, 1975.

———. *Sor Juana Inés de la Cruz, o, Las trampas de la fe*. Barcelona: Seix Barral, 1982.

———. *Vuelta*. Barcelona: Seix Barral, 1976.

Paz, Octavio, et al., eds. *Poesía en movimiento: México, 1915-1966*. Mexico: Siglo Veintiuno, 1970.

Perdigó, Luisa M. *La estética de Octavio Paz*. Madrid: Playor, 1975.

Persin, Margaret H. "Chaos, Order and Meaning in the Poetry of Octavio Paz." *Revista canadiense de estudios hispánicos*, 4 (1980), 155-68.

Pezzoni, Enrique. " 'Blanco': La respuesta al deseo." In *Aproximaciones a Octavio Paz*, edited by Angel Flores. Mexico: Joaquín Mortiz, 1974. 237-53.

Phillips, Rachel. *The Poetic Modes of Octavio Paz*. London: Oxford Univ. Press, 1972.

Poulet, Georges, *Les métamorphoses du cercle*. Paris: Plon, 1961.

Rawson, Philip. *Tantra: The Indian Cult of Ecstasy*. New York: Avon, 1973.

Richer, Jean. *Gérard de Nerval et les doctrines ésotériques*. Paris: Editions du Griffon d'or, 1947.

Ríos, Julián, and Octavio Paz. *Solo a dos voces*. Barcelona: Editorial Lumen, 1973.

Rodman, Selden. "Octavio Paz." In *Tongues of Fallen Angels: Conversations with Jorge Luis Borges [and others]*. New York: New Directions, 1974, 135-61.

Rodríguez Monegal, Emir. "Relectura de *El arco y la lira*." *Revista iberoamericana*, 37 (1971), 35-46.

Bibliography 185

Rodríguez Padrón, Jorge. *Octavio Paz*. Madrid: Ediciones Júcar, 1975.

Roggiano, Alfredo, ed. *Octavio Paz*. Madrid: Editorial Fundamentos, 1979.

———. "Persona y ámbito de Octavio Paz." In *Octavio Paz*. Madrid: Editorial Fundamentos, 1979, 5-33.

Sahagún, Fray Bernardino de. *Historia general de las cosas de Nueva España*. 5 vols. Mexico: Robredo, 1938.

Sánchez, Porfirio. "Imágenes y metafísica en la poesía de Octavio Paz: La negación del tiempo y del espacio." *Cuadernos americanos*, 29 (1970), 149-59.

Sánchez Robayna, Andrés. "Regreso y fundación" [*Vuelta*]. In *Octavio Paz*, edited by Alfredo Roggiano. Madrid: Editorial Fundamentos, 1979, 361-69.

Seabrook, Roberta. "La poesía en movimiento: Octavio Paz." *Revista iberoamericana*, 37 (1971), 161-75.

———. "Vrindaban." In *Aproximaciones a Octavio Paz*, edited by Angel Flores. Mexico: Joaquín Mortiz, 1974, 189-99.

Soustelle, Jacques. *La Pensée cosmologique des anciens mexicains*. Paris: Hermann & Cie., 1940.

Sucre, Guillermo. " 'Blanco': Un archipiélago de signos." In *Aproximaciones a Octavio Paz*, edited by Angel Flores. Mexico: Joaquín Mortiz, 1974, 232-36.

———. "La fijeza y el vértigo." *Revista iberoamericana*, 37 (1971), 47-72.

Wilson, Jason. *Octavio Paz: A Study of His Poetics*. Cambridge: Cambridge Univ. Press, 1979.

Xirau, Ramón. *Octavio Paz: El sentido de la palabra*. Mexico: Joaquín Mortiz, 1970.

———. "Octavio Paz, poeta de la participación." In *Poetas de México y España*. Madrid: Ediciones José Porrúa Turanzas, 1962. 148-56.

———. "Octavio Paz y los caminos de la transparencia." In *Poesía y conocimiento*. Mexico: Joaquín Mortiz, 1978, 92-136.

———. "Pasado en claro." *La gaceta* (Mexico), 62 (Feb. 1976), 8.

Yurkievich, Saúl. "Octavio Paz, indagador de la palabra." *Revista iberoamericana*, 37 (1971), 73-95.

Zaid, Gabriel. *Leer poesía*. Mexico: Joaquín Mortiz, 1972.

———. "Significaciones últimas." *La cultura en México* (supplement of *Siempre*), 287, 16 Aug. 1967, 6.

Index

Note: Only the titles of works by Octavio Paz are indexed separately.